DISCOVER
CROSS STITCH

DISCOVER
CROSS STITCH

40 ORIGINAL PROJECTS TO BUILD YOUR NEEDLECRAFT SKILLS

STEVEN JENKINS
AND
JANE FRANKLIN

HAMLYN

First published in Great Britain in 1994 by Hamlyn
an imprint of Reed Consumer Books Limited
Michelin House, 81 Fulham Road London SW3 6RB
and Auckland, Melbourne, Singapore and Toronto

TEXT AND PHOTOGRAPHS © 1994
REED INTERNATIONAL BOOKS LIMITED

CROSS STITCH DESIGNS © 1994 **STEVEN JENKINS**

SERIES EDITOR: **JONATHAN HILTON**
SERIES ART EDITOR: **PRUE BUCKNELL**
ART EDITOR: **ALISON SHACKLETON**
EXECUTIVE EDITOR: **JUDITH MORE**
ART DIRECTOR: **JACQUI SMALL**

PHOTOGRAPHS BY: **LUCY MASON**

ISBN: 0 60058 305 8

DTP ALISON SHACKLETON
ORIGINATION BY MANDARIN, SINGAPORE
PRINTED AND BOUND IN BARCELONA, SPAIN BY CAYFOSA

CONTENTS

INTRODUCTION

Cross stitch was not devised by a single person in a single place at a single time. Instead, it probably developed in many parts of the world, beginning thousands of years ago. It is easy to imagine that, given some of the coarsely woven fabrics available in earlier times, a simple darning exercise or the desire to put an identifying mark on a garment, could lead to more extravagant decoration using threads coloured with different vegetable dyes.

Traditional crafts such as cross stitch tend to develop slowly, with techniques and materials being refined over generations. As fabrics became finer, so the skill of the stitcher would have increased. Decorated garments, pictures and wall hangings would have demonstrated family skills to visitors and, as a means of passing on these skills, the cross stitch sampler evolved and became a true folk-art form crossing both cultural and social boundaries.

Although cross stitch has been with us for a long time, its popularity has fluctuated with the changing fashions over the generations. In the early 19th century there was a great revival of cross stitch as many of the diligently worked samplers and pictures that we see in antique shops today testify. Each of these samplers has a story to tell about the person who worked it, their lifestyle and interests. If we know who actually stitched them, if perhaps they have been passed down as heirlooms through one family, then that story becomes even more fascinating.

In our own century and right up until the 1950s, it was quite usual for many women to spend their leisure hours eagerly cross stitching. Now, having skipped almost a whole generation, this creative and satisfying pastime is back, more popular than ever, and showing every sign that it will continue for a long while to come.

Here in this book we have tried to present a wide variety of designs that will appeal to today's generation of cross stitchers. You won't find a plethora of cute "fluffy kittens"

or solid "old master" portraits or landscapes. To help encourage and inspire you to greater things, we have put together a wide range of contemporary designs, using as many different techniques as possible.

Cross stitch is a form of embroidery where you either count the threads in your fabric to place your stitches or sew over a printed design. In this book, we are dealing with the former, which is often called counted cross stitch. But forget the crude work you may remember doing at school: cross stitch is capable of producing very sophisticated results. To demonstrate this there is a selection of up-dated samplers, from small, starter projects through to full-scale exercises. And we have not forgotten the importance of presentation. Our designs for cards, key rings and paperweights are easy to stitch and, when completed, make ideal personal accessories or gifts for family and friends.

All attractive and useful projects in themselves, each of the cross stitch exercises is intended to act as a springboard for your ideas. You can substitute your choice of colours, for example, for the suggested ones, or you can take a part of a design and apply it to something else. You can see examples of this type of substitution in the starry throw project on pages 44-5 or the key fobs on pages 76-7. Once you have learned the fundamental methods and techniques and acquired the necessary skills and confidence, you can then "break the rules" as you see fit.

Discover Cross Stitch aims to present new ideas – ideas which, when coupled with the exciting thread colours and the wide range of accessories available today, will help you to bring a fresh perception to this age-old craft. Above all we want to help you enjoy yourself as you make the most of this rewarding craft. We would like to think that you will create a treasured heirloom that will be enjoyed by generations of your family yet to be born.

MATERIALS AND TECHNIQUES

For those new to cross stitch there may be references to threads, types of stitches, materials, equipment and some techniques that you are not familiar with. The following pages go into detail explaining some of terms and techniques you will encounter.

FABRICS

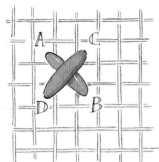

Cross stitch on evenweave

Counted cross stitch is worked on fabrics that have easily discernible vertical and horizontal threads. These fabrics are usually of two types: blockweaves, such as aida and binca; or evenweaves, such as linen.

BLOCKWEAVES

Cross stitch on blockweave

Blockweaves look as if they are woven from thin strips of material. Where the vertical and horizontal strips cross, they form a square with a hole at each corner. Cross stitches are formed by using these holes to sew through, and each single stitch thus sits neatly over a single block (*see left*).

Since they are so easy to use, blockweaves are the most popular fabric for counted cross stitch, and they are available with different numbers of holes per inch (hpi). The number of holes per inch determines how many stitches you can make per inch, and it is this that dictates the size and delicacy of your stitched piece. The complete range of sizes runs from 6

hpi binca to 22 hpi aida. There are also a range of linens, from very coarse to quite fine, so you have a lot of scope when it comes to choosing the fabric to work on.

For many cross stitchers, 14 hpi aida is a favourite. The squares are big enough to work easily, yet small enough to give good design detail. Binca, which is a good fabric for children, also lends itself to advanced projects, and should not be overlooked.

However, blockweaves can also be sized not by their hpi but by the number of squares per inch – known as the "count". To all intents and purposes, there is no difference between squares and holes per inch, and if you come across the term 14 count aida, for example, it is exactly the same as 14 hpi aida.

EVENWEAVES

Evenweaves have the same number of threads running vertically and horizontally. But since they are not woven in blocks they are not as easy to work on as blockweaves. Each stitch is usually worked over two vertical and two horizontal threads (*see left*), and since you have to decide on these yourself, you need to be very accurate with your counting.

Linen is a lovely fabric to work on, but it is expensive. However, you can buy evenweaves in cotton and rayon mixtures and both give very good results.

One fabric that looks like a blockweave but is, in fact, an evenweave, is hardanger, which is woven in pairs of threads and looks as if it is made up of blocks.

CANVAS

There are three main types of canvas: single (mono) canvas, woven from single threads; interlocked canvas, woven from threads that are locked at the intersections (*see right*); and double (Penelope) canvas (*see right*), which has pairs of threads running horizontally and vertically.

Single and interlocked are graded according to the number of threads per inch, and double by the number of holes. There is a good choice of size, ranging from 22 gauge, for very fine work in cottons, to 7 gauge, for work in wool.

PLAINWEAVES

Since they are so densely woven, many plainweaves are not suitable for counted cross stitch. However, by using waste canvas you can embroider "impossible" fabrics – such as cotton sheeting, denim, silk or jersey – with ease. Waste canvas is a special double canvas recognizable by the blue threads running through it. It is loosely woven and held together with water-soluble glue. To use it, cut off a piece larger than your design and tack it firmly to the material. Then, stitch over the waste canvas as if you were cross stitching ordinary double

canvas, but go through the plainweave material as well. Stitches should be firmly placed, but not too tight.

When finished, trim off the excess canvas, dampen the whole area to dissolve the glue bonding the threads, and pull them out from behind the stitches.

KNITTED FABRICS

To work on fine knitted fabric, use the waste canvas method. Larger knits can be used directly as a background for counted cross stitch – you simply need to get your eye in. If you look at stocking stitch, you will see that each stitch looks a little heart shaped. With some imagination, transform that heart into a square, like the blocks you see on blockweaves. You then make one cross stitch over each knitted stitch.

Sometimes, the stitches are longer than they are wide, so do a test by counting stitches up and across. If there is too much variation in the number of stitches along and number of rows up, the design may distort. If so, use the waste canvas method.

Knitted fabrics can stretch, so it may be best to tack interlining behind the design area before starting. Then cross stitch your design through both knitting and interlining. When you have finished, cut off any excess interlining from around the design area. The interlining that is left acts as a permanent backing to your design and holds the knitting stable when you wear and wash the garment.

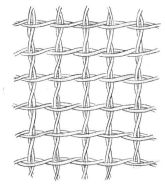

Interlocked canvas

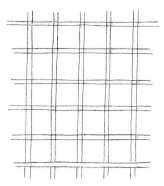

Double canvas

Metallic thread

Stranded cotton

Coton à broder

Marlitt

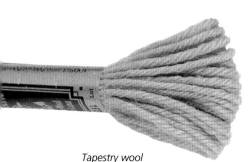

Cotton perle

Tapestry wool

THREADS

In early samplers and cross stitch, silks and wools were popular threads. But as each generation has taken up this craft, so devotees have used the materials that were most easily accessible at that time.

STRANDED COTTON

The most popular thread today is stranded cotton. This is available in a wide range of more than 300 colours and, on the whole, is very economical to use.

Before starting to work, cut the lengths of cotton you need and separate them into their component 6 strands. Then work with the required number of strands – however many needed to give good coverage. If you are still learning, trying to keep a consistent tension and an even finish, it is best to practise with the standard combination of two strands of cotton on 14 hpi aida.

When it is worked, stranded cotton has a dull shine. Knowing this, you can create a variety of effects by working with different numbers of threads on the one design. For example, to get the effect of distance or shadow, work the foreground in two strands and the background in one.

STRANDED SILK

Silk is more expensive and has fewer colours than stranded cotton, but it gives a richer and deeper finish. Work stranded silk in the same way as stranded cotton, or mix the two in the same design. Marlitt can be substituted for stranded silk.

FLOWER THREAD

Cotton flower thread is not divisible and is softer than stranded cotton. Although the range of colours is not as extensive as with cotton thread, its palette is more natural and earthy. There are bright colours as well, but the thread's matt finish means that it works very well with linens and evenweaves to give an antique or country flavour to your work.

PERLE COTTON

This is a thick and wonderfully silky thread. Again there is a large range of colours and you can buy it by the skein or on card reels. Perle cotton is ideal for chunky borders or abstract designs and always gives a richness to your designs.

SOFT EMBROIDERY COTTON

This is rather like a chunky version of a flower thread – the sort of thing that you might have experimented with at school when you first learned to stitch. It has an even, matt sheen, and some of the canvas projects in this book would work very well on a small-gauge canvas using this thread.

METALLIC THREAD

This is, for the most part, composed of fine strips of metal, such as aluminium. The weights and thicknesses of this thread vary greatly and there are always new ones appearing on the market. Gold, silver, bronze and copper are the most popular colours. Metallic threads are well worth experimenting with – the Christmas stocking project on pages 52-3, for example, would be a good candidate.

WOOL

Wool is one of the most adaptable and enduring of threads. The two basic weights for cross stitch are crewel and tapestry. Crewel is the finer of the two and works well on linens and natural fabrics. In this book the tapestry weight has been used for the canvas and plastic canvas work. If you want to use crewel wool instead, practise with combining two or three lengths where its is recommended that you use one length of tapestry wool.

Knitting wool in 4-ply or double knit can be used for cross stitch. Try to avoid acrylic or acrylic/wool mixes, since these may "bobble".

BEADING

This popular Victorian technique has once again appeared to become one of the more exciting techniques used by today's stitchers. You will find that there are many projects available that call for dense bead work, and others in which the design is in cross stitch and beads are used to provide detail and highlighting.

DIFFERENT TYPES OF STITCH

All of the projects in this book can be undertaken using just a small number of different stitches, most of which you will already be familiar with.

CROSS STITCH

A cross stitch is made in two movements, from two diagonal stitches crossing over each other. The result is a symmetrical, almost square, stitch. If working on a block-weave, the stitch lies over one block; on an evenweave, it lies over a block made from two horizontal and two vertical threads.

To work one cross stitch, bring the needle up through the fabric at A and across and down at B (*see left*). This gives the underneath half of the stitch. Then, bring your needle up at C and down again at D for the top half of the stitch. The front of your work shows a whole stitch; the back two vertical stitches.

In most instances you will be able to work in rows, not in individual stitches. Not only is this easier and quicker to do, it also gives a more even finish to your work. First, work all the underneath half of the stitches (*see below*). Then return, working the top half of the stitches.

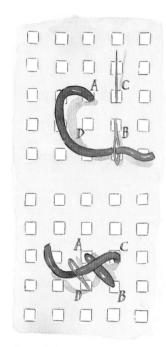

Cross stitch

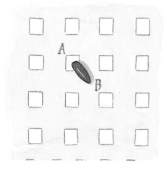

Half cross stitch

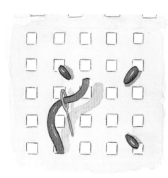

Quarter stitch

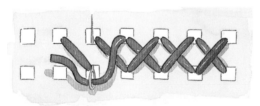

Row of cross stitches

HALF CROSS STITCH

Sometimes you may need half cross stitches – perhaps for an area of shading. Stitches should go in the same direction, or the work will look uneven. Get into the habit of working them in the same direction.

QUARTER STITCH

These are very small stitches and are usually made to fill in gaps – in making three-quarter cross stitches, for example. Quarter stitches are worked from the corner of a block to the centre (*see left*).

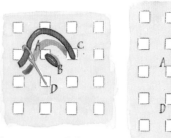

Three-quarter stitch

THREE-QUARTER STITCH

Three-quarter stitches are made from a combination of quarter and half stitches and are used for adding detail. Work the quarter stitch first (*see above*), from A in the corner to B in the middle. Then work the half stitch from C to D. The quarter block not worked can be left or filled in with the colour of the surrounding area.

BACK STITCH

These are usually worked in one strand, if you are using stranded thread. Back stitches are often used for outlining and should be done after the cross stitching. They appear on the front of the work as a smooth line.

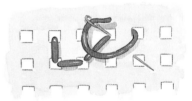

Back stitch

FRENCH KNOT

To make a French knot, bring the needle up through the fabric, keeping the thread taut (*see right*). Twist the needle around the thread, once, twice or three times, depending on the size knot. Push the needle through the fabric close to where it emerged. When halfway through, pull the thread tight, making the knot, and push the needle and thread to the back.

LONG STITCH

A quick way of filling in background is with long stitches. The stitches can be vertical, horizontal or diagonal and, unlike back stitch, they can cover more than one block of fabric (*see right*).

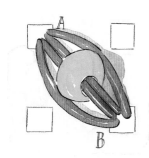

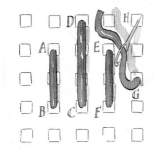

Fixing beads

FIXING BEADS

Traditionally, beads are fixed to the design by a half cross stitch (*see opposite*). Bring your needle to the front where you want the bead, as if forming an ordinary half cross stitch. Pick up the bead with the needle and thread it on to the yarn. Pull the yarn through and make sure the bead sits well on the fabric. Then complete the half cross stitch.

However good your tension, using this method beads will tend to wobble on the finished item. To prevent this happening there is an alternative method. Use either sewing cotton or the yarn you are cross stitching with, and double it so that you are working with two strands (*see left*). Fix the thread to the back of your work and pull it through to the front where you want the bead to be. Pick up the bead and finish the half cross stitch, as above.

Then, bring the needle through at A again, take the thread over the top of the bead so that one strand lies on the left of it and one on the right, and complete the half cross stitch. This second stitch on either side of the bead anchors it firmly in position and makes your work more even.

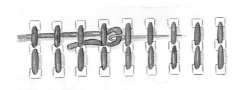

STARTING AND FINISHING

When starting or finishing a piece of work, the thread should not be secured on the back of the material with a knot because this may show through on the right side. To start, either run your new thread behind the stitches you have already worked, or hold the last 1in (2.5cm) of your thread behind your work and make sure it is secured by your new stitching. To finish, run your thread carefully through the backs of the stitches you have already worked (*see below*).

French knot

Long stitch

Starting and finishing

SIZES

One of the fascinating things about counted cross stitch is that, once you have a charted design, you can work it on any count fabric you like without having to do any complicated recalculations. Whatever count you choose, the design will look the same – just smaller or larger, depending on whether you have chosen fabric with fewer or more hpi.

With a little basic arithmetic, you can work out your design area quite easily. For example, if your design is 126 stitches wide, it will be 9in wide if you work on 14 hpi fabric. In other words, if there are 14 stitches to the inch, you need 9in to work 126 stitches, or $126 \div 14 = 9$.

Work the same design on 16 hpi fabric, however, and it will be approximately 8in wide ($126 \div 16 = 7.875$). So the rule is: divide the number of stitches by the hpi to obtain the size in inches.

NEEDLES

There are no hard and fast rules regarding the size of the needles you should use for each fabric but, generally speaking, a size 24 needle (blunt ended) is best for medium-gauge work; a tapestry needle is necessary for the canvas and plastic canvas projects; and a number 8 crewel is recommended on finer linens and 18 count aida. Obviously if your needle distorts the fabric at all, or leaves a gaping hole, then choose a smaller size. On the other hand, don't use a needle that is too small on canvas projects, since this will damage the threads and give you poor coverage of the canvas.

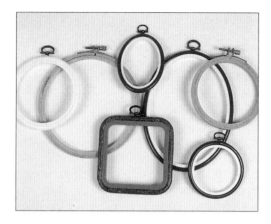

HOOPS AND FRAMES

Some cross stitchers prefer to work with the fabric stretched taut in a frame or hoop (*see above*) in order to achieve an even tension; others prefer the freedom of working with the fabric loose. Embroidery hoops are the traditional equipment for lightweight fabrics but, especially on smaller projects, you can use a flexi-hoop (*see opposite*). A tapestry frame may be useful if you are working on a large piece of material but it is not very portable and, since setting it up takes quite a while, it might actually dampen your enthusiasm. The best advice is to experiment to find the method you are most comfortable with. Start off with a small hoop and, if it seems unsuccessful or awkward, try without it. Remember, it is very important that you enjoy your stitching. Finally, if you do work with a hoop, the fabric will definitely need washing afterward because the hoop will leave a "shadow image" behind.

PREPARING FABRIC

Work out the size of your design and add on at least 2in (5cm) all around before you cut your fabric. For example, for a design measuring 8 x 10in (20 x 25cm) you need to cut the fabric to 10 x 12in (25 x 30cm). To prevent it fraying, you can edge the fabric with blanket stitching, tack all the way around with ordinary sewing thread or hem the piece.

Next, fold the fabric in half both vertically and horizontally and tack along these folds in a thread colour that will show clearly, marking the middle lines. Where they cross is the centre of the fabric and this is where you will usually begin stitching your design. You will have to remove these stitched lines when you have finished your work, so remember not to sew through, or too tightly over, them while you are working your design.

If you are working with canvas, bind the edges with masking tape and then mark the middle with an indelible pen. For projects worked on plastic canvas, cut the canvas neatly with sharp scissors and carefully trim off any spikes to leave your work smooth-edged.

USING THREADS

The thread you use often suggests the best method of working. For example, if you are using wool, cut what you need from the ball or skein as required, restricting yourself to 15-16in (40cm) lengths to prevent tangles. If the wool starts to unwind as you are stitching, simply tie it off at the back and start stitching again with the other end of the wool that is still intact. With stranded cotton, and most other threads, 8in (20cm) lengths are about right – you will not have to rethread too often and they should not become tangled. If the thread does start to twist, simply hold the fabric and let the needle and thread hang down loosely to unwind.

THREAD ORGANIZER

If you are working with a large number of threads and are worried about mixing up similar colours, consider using a thread organizer. You can easily make one yourself by punching a strip of cardboard with holes. Cut a couple of lengths of a particular colour thread, feed them through one of the holes, and write that colour's number alongside it. Repeat this process with each colour you are using in the design.

When you divide your threads, the individual strands can be safely stored on the thread organizer until needed. This method saves you the bother and annoyance of hunting around the room for all those oddments of thread and also helps you to avoid the dreaded workbox tangles.

FINISHING

When you have completed a project, the chances are that it will have picked up odd bits of dirt and dust along the way. Washing it before mounting will remove this grime and show off your stitching to the best possible effect.

WASHING

Use lukewarm water and mild soap powder. Rinse it thoroughly in cool water and, should any of the colours look like running, keep rinsing it until you are sure it has stopped. If you don't, you may be left with ghostly shadows around the strong colours.

USING A FLEXI-HOOP

Flexi-hoops are a quick and easy way of finishing and presenting your work. There are two hoops; the inner hoop is made of a rigid material and the outer, more flexible ring, is stretched over it. Pull the hoops apart and, using the inner ring as a template, cut a piece of backing felt, or some other fabric, to fit the outside diameter. Place your washed stitching centrally over the inner ring and then refit the outer one, pulling it on from the front. Now adjust the position of your work by pulling the material by its edges. When satisfied, trim the excess fabric (*see below*) down to 1in (2.5cm).

Next, lay your backing felt or fabric over the back and, using a running stitch around the edge, cover the stitching on the rear of the design.

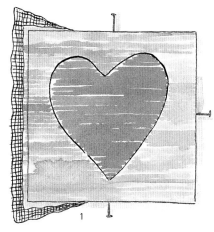

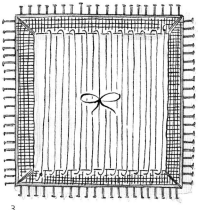

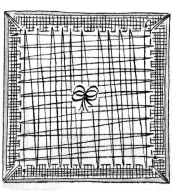

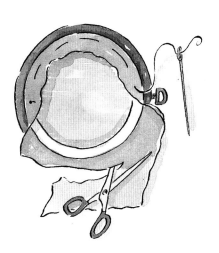

LACING AND FRAMING

Frames normally have a rebate in the back for the glass and a piece of cardboard. Cut a piece of card to fit this rebate, allowing for the thickness of the fabric as it folds around the sides. Leave extra space around the design since all frames, except clip-frames, overlap your work a little.

Place your work, face up, with the design centred over the card and fold the fabric around the back of the card. Place pins through the fabric and into the edge of the card at the middle of each side (1). Using more pins, ease the fabric around the card (2). Next, turn your work over and, with a needle, secure sewing cotton to the top corner of one of the side flaps. Then work down, sewing from side to side and from bottom to top, at 1in (2.5cm) intervals (3) Keep the thread taut enough to pull the fabric tight without distorting its shape. You will end up with a grid effect of threads.Remove the pins and you are ready to frame your work (4).

FINISHING TIPS

● After washing in mild detergent, lay a thick towel on an ironing board or table and place a tea towel or thin cloth over it.

● Gently squeeze – do not wring – your work, place it on top of the towel with the design face down, and press it with a warm iron. The towel cushions your work, preventing the stitching from being squashed flat.

● Iron out any creases in the fabric and, when it's dry, your work will be ready for lacing (*see left*).

MAKING UP CUSHIONS

Many of the projects in this book would make excellent cushions, which are a perfect showcase for displaying your stitching.

First, choose a backing fabric that will contrast, or co-ordinate, with your stitching. Then decide what opening method you are going to use to allow for washing at some later date. If you choose a zip, place this along a centre seam and secure it, making sure that it will open on the outside of the cushion. An alternative to a zip is the button back, where three button holes with covered buttons create the centre seam. Finally, there is the folded overlap, which avoids any complicated sewing.

BASIC TECHNIQUE
Place the right sides of your stitching and backing together and pin them round the edge of the stitching, or a marked-out edge if there is an allowance of fabric around the design. It is always best to leave a "breathing space" around an open design

(where not all the fabric is stitched), since cropping in too close might spoil the effect. With a fully stitched piece, the design will go right up to the edge of the finished cushion.

Working outward from the centre seam, sew securely along the outside edges. Cut these outside edges to within about ½in (1cm) of the canvas or fabric, cutting the corners at 45° to give a neater edge when it is finished. When you do turn the work inside out, ease out these corners with a pencil for a really expert finish.

To add the final detail, you can sew a piece of braid or cord around the edge of the cushion, but remember to buy a little more than you think you need – the corners always seem to use up more than you expect. Start the cord halfway along one side, not at a corner, since this will help you to disguise the join more effectively. Alternatively, you can add piping to finish off your cushion's edges, as was done on the tile cushion project seen on pages 38-9.

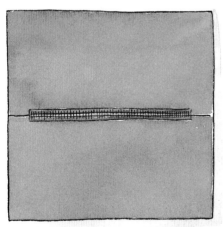

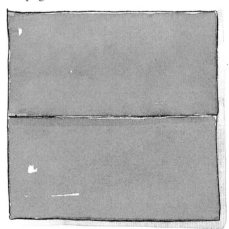

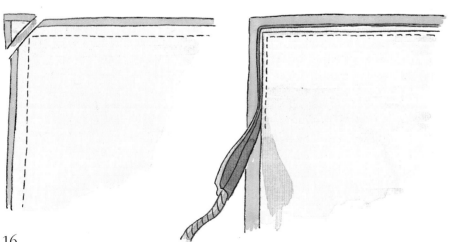

USING THE CHARTS

Each square on the charts accompanying the projects in this book represents one complete cross, or X-shaped, stitch, and the accompanying colour bars give the Anchor colour reference numbers used in the example piece. To find out the DMC equivalents of these, see pages 108-9. A full square represents a whole cross stitch and where two colours occupy the same square then one is a quarter stitch and the other is a three-quarter stitch. To control the colour balance of your work, stitch the colour you want to give more prominence to in the three-quarter stitch.

Some cross stitchers like to work all the stitches of one colour before starting the others. However, this can lead to mistakes when you have a large area to cover. It is better, therefore, to work each small area of one colour and then change the thread to work the adjacent stitches in the next colour. For example, you might work one petal of a flower and then change colour to stitch the centre, and so on. Building up the design in this way will help to make

sure that the finished piece is accurately worked. You may like to use a ruler or a piece of card to mark off each area of the chart as you complete it, and only concentrate on one section of it at a time.

DISPLAYING YOUR WORK

Many craft supply shops, wool and embroidery specialists and mail order outlets dealing with craft materials often carry a large range of "blanks" into which your finished cross stitch pieces can be inserted (*see above*). Many of the projects featured in this book make use of these products and, once they are assembled, your stitching will look indistinguishable from that produced by a professional craft worker.

If you intend to use one of these for your stitching, first buy the one you want and then size your design so that it will fit comfortably within the display area of that particular piece. Each comes with complete assembly instructions.

Just a few examples of the hundreds available are shown here and you will need to obtain a catalogue to see all your options.

MATERIALS

Fabric: 12 x 13in (30.5 x 33cm)
11 hpi aida, white or cream

Needle

Thread: 2 skeins of each
colour. Use 2 strands for the
cross stitch

INSTRUCTIONS

Number of stitches: 90 x 110.
Finished design size: 8⅓ x 10in
(20.8 x 25.4cm) on 11 hpi aida.
Prepare your fabric (*see pp. 8-17*).
Find the centre of your material
and start stitching from the centre
of the design.

EASY LEVEL

NUMBERS AND LETTERS SAMPLERS

There are hundreds of styles of number and letters to choose from, and a few are given on pages 104-5. If you wish, take the examples illustrated here as your guide, copying both the style and colours; or borrow any of the elements and adapt them to suit your own particular design requirements.

Think about the colours of the numbers or letters, how they will work both within the design and the sampler's wider setting. Work the design out before beginning, using copies of the graph paper printed on pages 106-7. The two samplers here are the same design size and both have been stitched in 11 hpi aida, which really is the largest fabric you can use for anything described as a serious project.

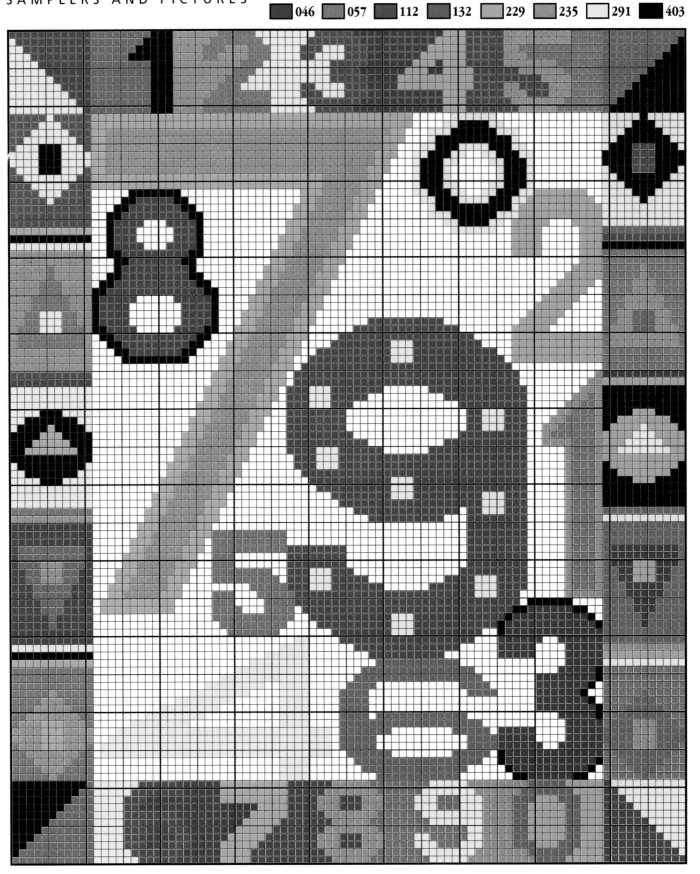

046 057 112 132 229 235 291 403

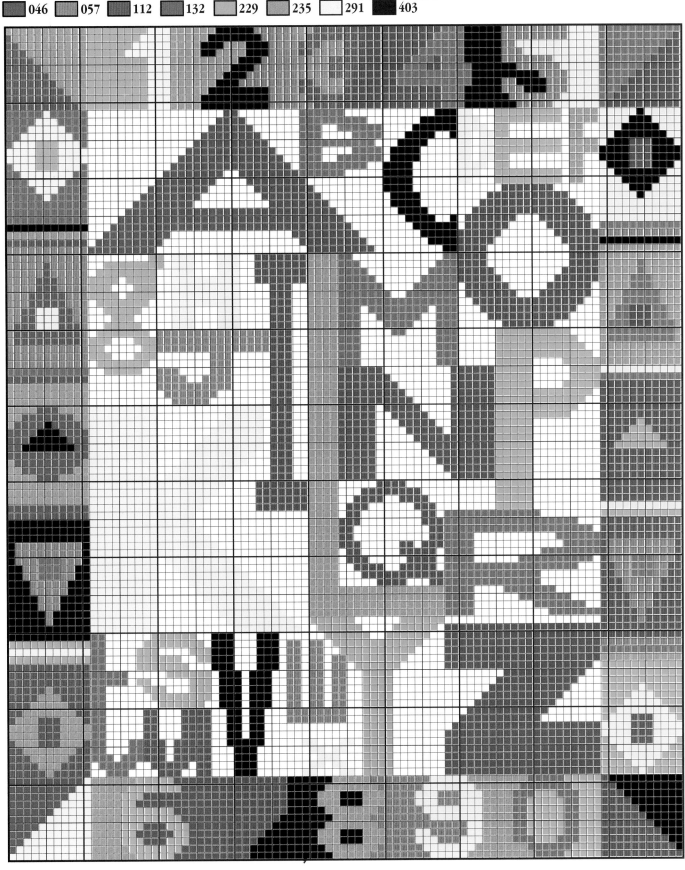

INSTRUCTIONS

Number of stitches: 140 x 162.
Finished design size: 7¾ x 9in
(19.5 x 22.8cm) on 18 hpi aida.
Start stitching 3in (7cm) from the
top of the fabric at the centre of
the design.

    Cut out a piece of cardboard
the same size as your stitched
fabric (1). Place the stitched work
face down with the cardboard
mount on top, making sure that
the card covers the design. Mitre
the corners and cut a cross in the
middle, as shown (2). Using
double-sided tape, secure the
outer sides and fold the inner
fabric over the card and stitch (3).
Make a backing piece and support
as shown. Glue this to the frame,
leaving an opening at the bottom
to slide a photograph through (4).

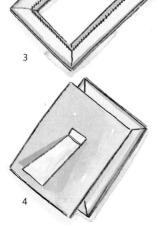

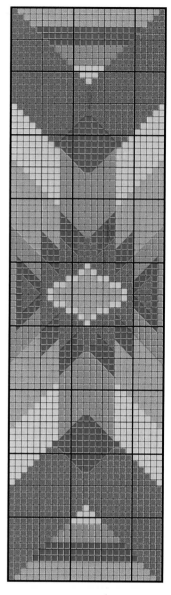

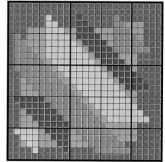

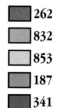

■	262
■	832
□	853
■	187
■	341

MATERIALS

Fabric: 11 x 12in
(28 x 30.5cm) 18 hpi aida

Needle

Thread: 3 skeins of each
colour. Use 2 strands for the
cross stitch

ETHNIC FRAME

Brightly coloured rugs and hangings are used by different cultures throughout the world. From India and Asia to Europe and the Americas, styles may vary but the desire to bring rich colours together with robust patterns seems to be universal.

Taking an ethnic theme as a starting point, this decorative frame brings a taste of foreign lands into your home. As well as using it to frame a suitable photograph, it would also make a particularly attractive mirror surround. Don't forget to have the glass sides ground smooth to remove those sharp edges that could cut into the stitching or backing material.

To reduce the overall size of the frame you could omit matching elements on each side. Tack out the edge of the design area in a contrasting thread colour before starting. Don't stitch through this thread, since it will have to be removed before making up.

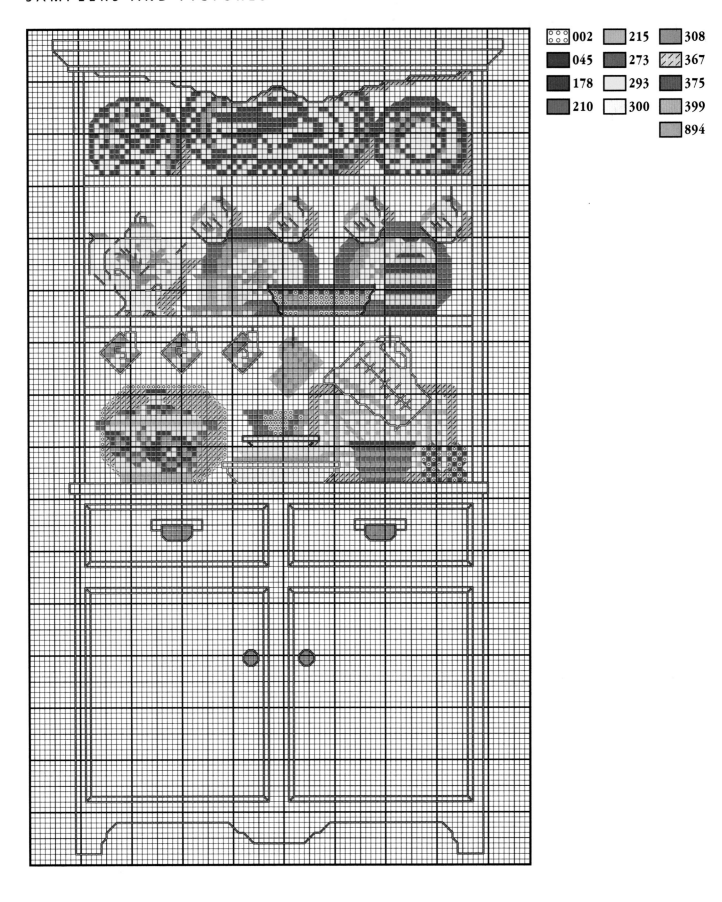

○○○ 002	215	308
045	273	╱╱ 367
178	293	375
210	300	399
		894

MATERIALS

Fabric: 13 x 8in (33 x 20.3cm)
18 hpi Rustico aida

Needle

Thread: 2 skeins of each
colour. Use 2 strands for the
cross stitch and 2 strands for
the back stitch

INSTRUCTIONS

Number of stitches: 157 x 88.
Finished design size: 8¾ x 5in
(22.3 x 12.5cm) on 18 hpi aida.
Prepare your fabric (*see pp. 8-17*),
find the centre of your fabric and
start stitching from the centre of
the design.

INTERMEDIATE LEVEL

DRESSER SAMPLER

The dresser is part of many people's
"ideal" kitchen. But don't worry if you
have not got the room – this cross
stitch version will fit into any size
kitchen. Based on a dresser cascading
with crockery, this sampler will display
your stitching talents to the full.

To allow you to concentrate on the
crockery, the dresser has been kept to a
simple outline of back stitches. If you
want to fit more on the dresser, double
its width to make it into a four-drawer,
four-cupboard model. If you do, remember to remove the middle upright.

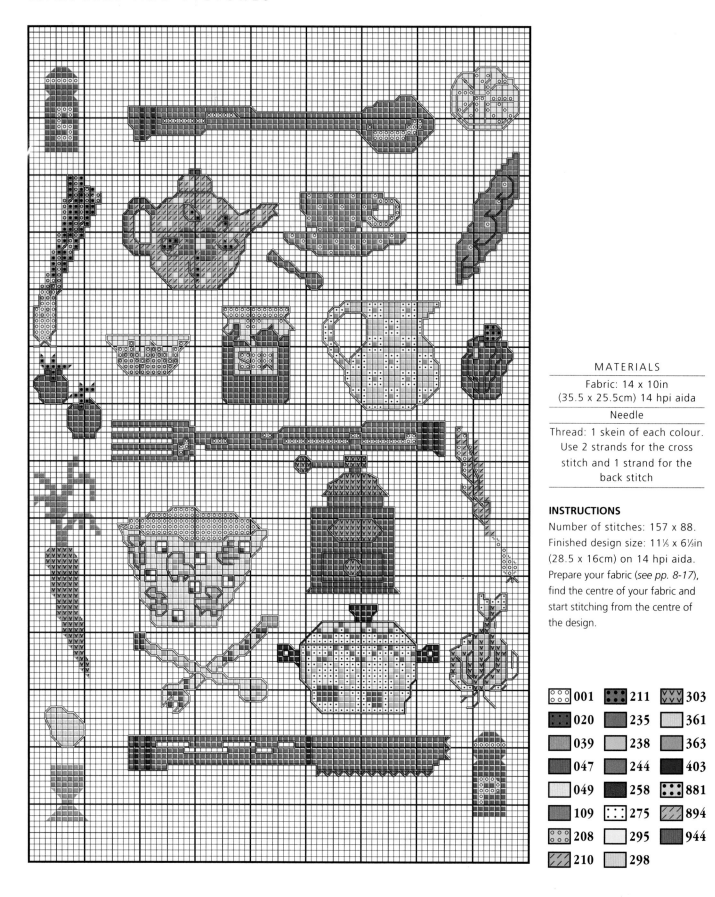

MATERIALS

Fabric: 14 x 10in
(35.5 x 25.5cm) 14 hpi aida

Needle

Thread: 1 skein of each colour.
Use 2 strands for the cross
stitch and 1 strand for the
back stitch

INSTRUCTIONS

Number of stitches: 157 x 88.
Finished design size: 11⅛ x 6⅓in
(28.5 x 16cm) on 14 hpi aida.
Prepare your fabric (see pp. 8-17),
find the centre of your fabric and
start stitching from the centre of
the design.

001	211	303
020	235	361
039	238	363
047	244	403
049	258	881
109	275	894
208	295	944
210	298	

KITCHEN SAMPLER

Anything connected with the kitchen can be included on this sampler. In the middle of the design shown here, space has been left on the jam jar for you to include your initials, but you could just as easily stitch your full name, the date and the address of your home at the bottom of the design.

Feel free to substitute any of the suggested objects for ones you prefer. You could also take one or two of the motifs and use them on their own. They make excellent cut-outs – treat one with needlework finisher (*see pp. 92-3*), attach a magnet, and you have a perfect fridge magnet to hold your shopping list or notes to the family.

MATERIALS

Fabric: 8 x 8in (20.3 x 20.3cm)
18 hpi white aida

Needle

Thread: 2 skeins of each blue,
2 of white and 1 of each of
the other colours. Use 2
strands for the cross stitch

INSTRUCTIONS

Number of stitches: 99 x 99.
Finished design size: 5 x 5in
(12.7 x 12.7cm) on 18 hpi aida.
Prepare your fabric (see pp. 8-17).
Stitch the check section first,
starting at the bottom centre, and
leave at least a 3in (7.5cm) border
from the edge of the fabric.

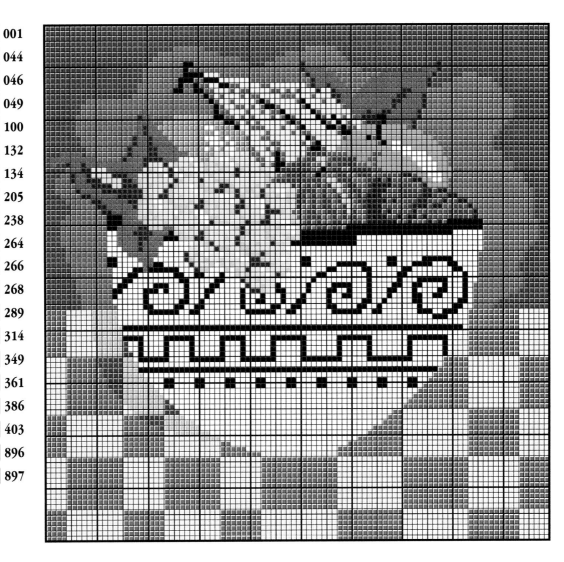

□	001
■	044
■	046
▨	049
■	100
■	132
■	134
■	205
▨	238
▨	264
■	266
■	268
▨	289
■	314
■	349
▨	361
□	386
■	403
■	896
■	897

INTERMEDIATE LEVEL

FRUIT BOWL PICTURE

Good enough to eat – that's what this cross stitch bowl overflowing with luscious fruit looks like. The fruit in this picture really comes to life when stitched at the size illustrated here.

Traditional cross stitch samplers often kept the objects depicted quite small, and this resulted in a lot of the background showing as plain material. Here, the approach is thoroughly modern – treating the fabric with an all-over technique, keeping to a single,

dominant subject, and mixing a palette of vividly coloured threads for the fruit as a contrast to the stark black and white of the fruit bowl.

One advantage of a design on this scale is that the three-dimensional effect really has impact, lifting the fruit and the bowl away from the background of bright squares. The disadvantage of this, however, is that there is a lot of careful, concentrated stitching required – but the results will more than justify all the effort you put in.

To create a really dramatic finished result, you could mount the piece in an attractive wooden frame and then hand paint, or spray, in a bold colour that contrasts or co-ordinates with the fruit in the picture.

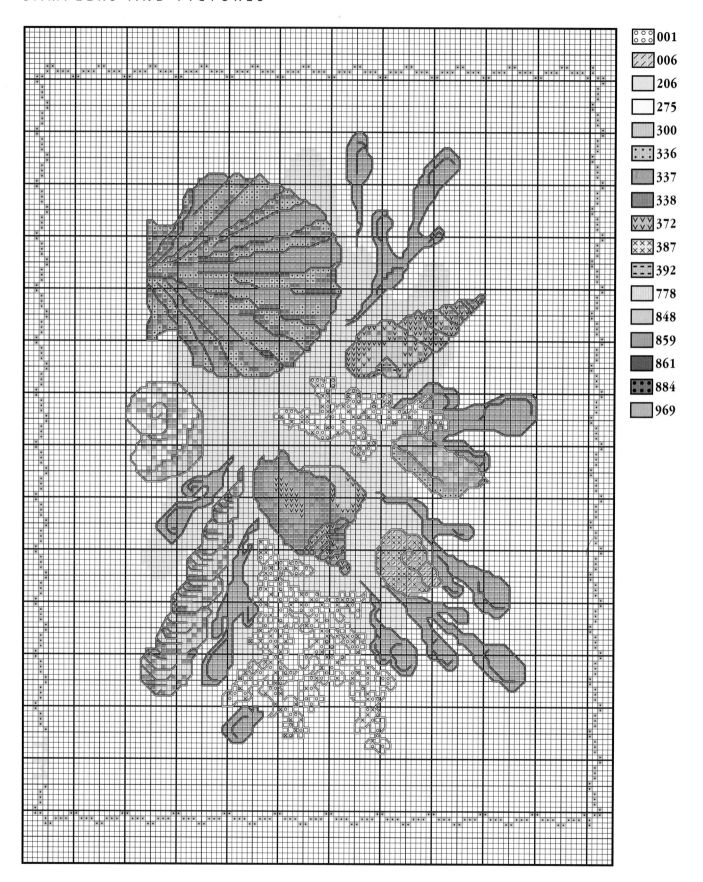

◦◦	001
▨	006
▢	206
▢	275
▨	300
⦂⦂	336
▨	337
▨	338
VVV	372
XXX	387
╌╌	392
▢	778
▢	848
▨	859
▨	861
▨	884
▨	969

SHELL PICTURE

Shells have an undeniable charm. In different cultures around the world shells have been used as jewellery, as currency and as natural decoration applied to such romantic features as the grottoes built in the grand gardens of 19th-century luminaries.

All of us can probably remember that as children how we would trawl up and down a sandy beach picking up handfuls of bright, wet and shiny shells. By the time we got them home, however, their lustre had usually faded, as if the life had gone from them. Now that we are older and wiser, we know that a coat of varnish would quickly restore their former brightness. But with this cross stitched picture, your shells will stay just as cheerful as the day you first worked them.

This collection of naturalistic shells worked in tranquil colours makes a satisfying cross stitch project and, as with many of the other sampler and picture projects in this chapter, individual designs can be easily lifted out and used as motifs on their own in tiny pictures. Alternatively, you could work them on to a set of bathroom towels to remind you of those pleasurable ambles along the sand.

If you like, you could mount your sampler in a suitable-sized clipframe and then decorate the edges of the glass with real shells glued into position. Don't forget that varnish though!

MATERIALS

Fabric: 11½ x 9in (29 x 23cm) 18 hpi ivory aida

Needle

Thread: 1 skein of each colour and 2 skeins of background colours. Use 1 strand for the cross stitch and 1 strand for the back stitch

INSTRUCTIONS

Number of stitches: 146 x 111. Finished design size: 8⅛ x 6⅛in (20.7 x 15.6cm) on 18hpi ivory aida.

Prepare your fabric (*see pp. 8-17*), find the centre of your fabric and start stitching from the centre of the design.

019
026
112
145
205
236
275
293
343

MATERIALS
Fabric: 11 x 13in (28 x 33cm)
16 hpi aida

Needle

Thread: 1 skein of each colour.
Use 1 strand for the cross
stitch and 1 strand for the
back stitch

INSTRUCTIONS
Number of stitches: 116 x 151.
Finished design size: 7¼ x 9½in
(18.5 x 14cm) on 16 hpi aida.
Prepare your fabric (*see pp. 8-17*),
find the centre of your fabric and
start stitching from the centre of
the design.

ADVANCED LEVEL

FESTIVAL SAMPLER

In the sampler pictured here you can probably see the design influences of the early 1950s, and all around is evidence of the new style introduced in that boom period following the war.

Here, you can see updated lettering and traditional sampler motifs used to create a vigorous mix of moving swirls, of numerals and alphabets, all anchored to the central star and coloured bar. To provide variety, there is also lots of back stitch to enhance the three-dimensional quality of the piece.

If you are inspired, extend the border down to give yourself more room and then include such information as names, anniversary dates or addresses, using the alphabets and numerals at the back of this book. You could also substitute any other motifs from this book or favourite ones of your own.

HOME ACCESSORIES

1014   175   123   306

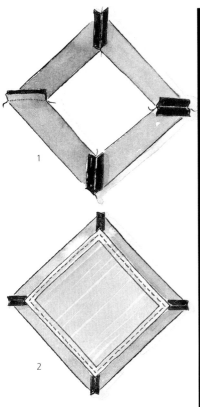

1

2

MATERIALS

Fabric: 10 x 10in
(25.4 x 25.4cm) 18 hpi aida

Contrasting/toning fabric
for making up

Needle

Thread: Stranded cotton – 4
skeins of each colour. Use 3
strands for the cross stitch

INSTRUCTIONS

Number of stitches: 125 x 125.
Finished design size: 7 x 7in
(17.8 x 17.8cm) on 18 hpi aida.
Prepare your fabric (*see pp. 8-17*),
find the centre of your fabric and
start stitching from the centre of
the design.

Cut four pieces of velvet and stitch
them together as shown (1), to
make a 4in (10cm) border around
the finished piece. Place the
finished piece face down over the
centre of the fabric border (2), and
stitch it to the inside edge of the
border, leaving one stitch all
around the cross stitch panel.

TILE CUSHION

The type of geometric patterns seen in
this piece can be found in the work of
many Victorian tile designers. You do
need to concentrate when working on
a symmetrically designed piece such as
this but, on the positive side, the
design is easy to stitch as long as you
keep your stitching and tension even.
The finished piece will look extremely
effective and, importantly, it will also
make a hard-wearing cushion cover.

As with many of the projects in this
book, you could easily adapt the
design to make an entirely different
piece, such as a table mat, or use just
part of the pattern to make a brooch
(*see pp. 92-3*). This same design would
make a stunning rug if it were worked
in wool on 7hpi canvas.

Either copy the colour scheme pictured above or, as always, look for your
inspiration elsewhere. You could
choose colours that co-ordinate with
your furniture, for example.

CHRISTMAS NAPKINS

This is one of the projects you will find in the book designed to get everyone into a festive, Christmas mood, looking forward to eating a sumptuous dinner from a well-decorated table. On such occasions, don't rely on paper towels; instead, use the designs illustrated here to make your own napkins, ones that you will enjoy using year after year.

There are three napkins pictured here, but you can increase this number to suit your needs, of course. Why not give different designs to members of your family to work up in plenty of time for Christmas dinner? They are all extremely simple to make and, with their Christmas themes of snowmen, holly and star motifs, very effective and stylish table accessories.

For a co-ordinated look, adapt the same motifs to make other decorations, such as a table centrepiece. And if you don't like tartan, use the waste canvas method (*see pp. 8-17*) to stitch on to any other festive fabric.

MATERIALS

Fabric: Tartan napkins Coats Patons Crafts supplied, or 12 x 12in (30.5 x 30.5cm) coloured aida

Needle

Thread: 1 skein of each colour. Use 2 strands for the cross stitch and 1 strand for the back stitch

INSTRUCTIONS

Number of stitches: 48 x 37 – maximum.
Finished design size: 3½ x 2⅝in (8.9 x 6.6cm) on 14 count panel aida.
Decide where you want the motifs to be positioned – centre, top left corner, and so on – and stitch according to the chart.

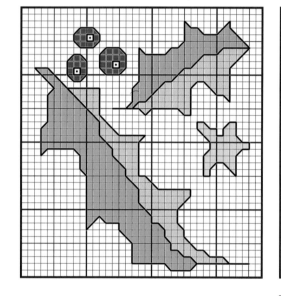

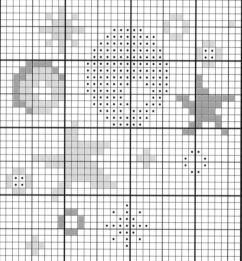

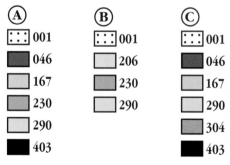

Ⓐ	Ⓑ	Ⓒ
001	001	001
046	206	046
167	230	167
230	290	290
290		304
403		403

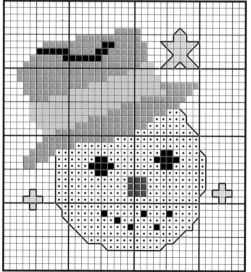

LEAF AND STAR MOTIF BOXES

These boxes are made with the cross stitcher specifically in mind and are produced with lids designed to display your stitched pieces (*see p. 17*). Made in ceramic, frosted glass or wood, they would make perfect trinket boxes for your dressing table.

The boxes come in a range of shapes and sizes and stitching a motif for one of the tiniest boxes takes no time at all. It is also an ideal way of using up all those oddments of thread you inevitably accumulate, so let the design be dictated by the thread colours you have available. The kaleidoscopic star motif is suitable for one of the larger round boxes and it would also make an ideal piece for a paperweight (*see pp. 50-1*).

Full instructions for mounting your work in the box lids comes with the boxes. If you are adapting another motif from the book, or using a design of your own, always allow a reasonable amount of space around your stitched design so that it does not look too cramped in the frame.

MATERIALS

Fabric (leaf): 5 x 5in (12.7 x 12.7cm) 14 hpi aida, white or cream

Fabric (star): 7 x 7in (17.8 x 17.8cm) 18 hpi aida

Needle

Thread: oddments of thread for the leaf box. Stranded cotton – 1 skein of each colour for the star box. Use 2 strands for the cross stitch

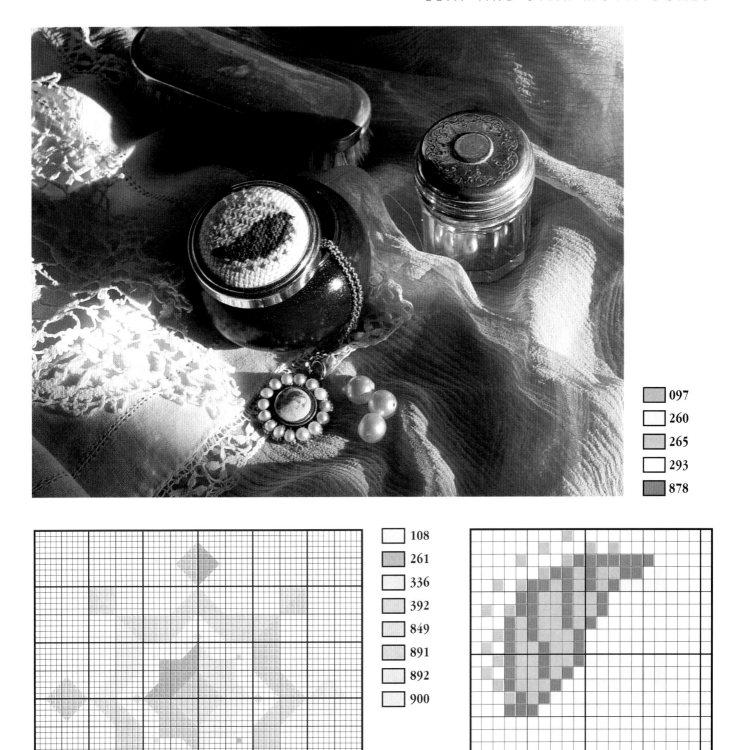

097
260
265
293
878

108
261
336
392
849
891
892
900

INSTRUCTIONS

Number of stitches (leaf): 19 x 18. Finished design size: 1⅜ x 1⅜in (4 x 4cm) on 14 hpi aida. Number of stitches (star): 56 x 56. Finished design size: 3 x 3in (7.6 x 7.6cm) on 18 hpi aida. Prepare your fabric (see pp. 8-17), find the centre of your fabric and stitch from the centre of the design.

STARRY THROW

Travellers in previous centuries often brought back bolts of exotic cloth from different parts of the world and draped them luxuriantly over their furniture. Now you can enjoy the same effect – without going to the ends of the earth to achieve it.

Rather than using just an ordinary piece of fabric to cover a chair or sofa, you can produce an ethnic-inspired design that will turn an inexpensive length of material into an exclusive throw. The fabric chosen for this example is plain, but you could just as easily pick a tartan, stripe or check.

Many furnishing fabrics come in 48in (1.2m) widths, so if you want to cover a large chair or sofa you may need to join two pieces together. Then you need to decide where you want to position the motifs. Because you cannot use ordinary stitching methods on these fabrics, the waste canvas method was used (*see pp. 8-17*). Upholstery braid will give the edges a professionally finished look, and the result is ideal for covering a piece of furniture that is showing a little wear and tear.

1

2

3

MATERIALS

Fabric: Fabric for the throw depends on size required, plus waste canvas

Needle

Thread: Stranded cotton – 1 skein of each colour for 2-3 motifs. Use 2 strands for the cross stitch

INSTRUCTIONS

Number of stitches: 23 x 23.
Finished design size: 2¾ x 2¾in (7 x 7cm) on 8-9 gauge waste canvas (*see pp. 8-17*).
Don't forget, before you start, always wash your fabric to avoid it shrinking or running.

Edge your chosen fabric and then position the waste canvas where you want the first design. Pin and tack it securely (1). Now you can stitch your chosen design, making sure you stitch through both the canvas and the fabric (2). Once you have finished one element of the design, simply repeat the process by tacking fresh waste canvas wherever you want to position the next motif.

Next, dampen each piece of canvas with a wet sponge to dissolve the glue, and then begin the process of removing all the strands of canvas. A pair of tweezers is what you need here (3). Pull out each canvas thread, but don't pull too hard or you could distort the design. If the canvas still seems too stiff, just dampen it again and gently ease out the threads. Sometimes the glue leaves a stain; if so, wash the throw before using it.

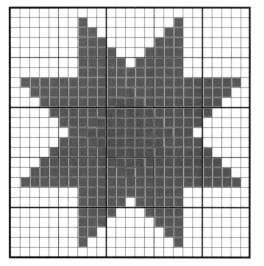

■ 922
■ 978

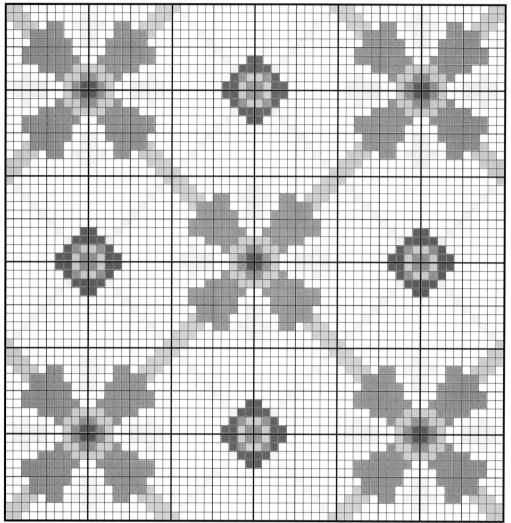

	288
	302
	330
	871
	879

MATERIALS

Fabric (small pincushion):
6 x 6in (15.2 x 15.2cm)
22 hpi aida

Fabric (large pincushions):
9 x 9in (22.8 x 22.8cm)
11 hpi aida

Needle

Thread: Stranded cotton – 1
skein of each colour. Use 2
strands for the cross stitch on
11 hpi aida and 1 strand on
22 hpi aida

INSTRUCTIONS

Number of stitches (small pincushion): 60 x 60.
Finished design size: 2¾ x 2¾in
(7 x 7cm) on 22 hpi aida.
Number of stitches (large pincushions): 60 x 60.
Finished design size: 5½ x 5½in
(14 x 14cm) on 11 hpi aida.
Prepare your fabric, find the centre
of your fabric and start stitching
from the centre of the design.

For additional information on
preparing fabric and making up
cushions, see pages 8-17.

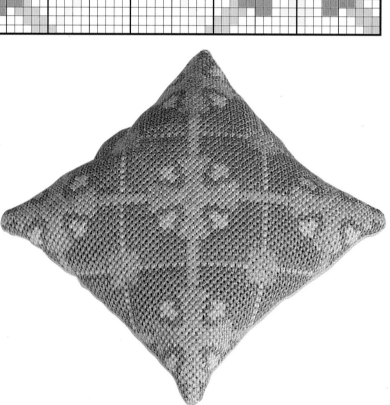

PINCUSHIONS

Tartans are enduring classic designs; there are literally hundreds of different patterns, and many have historic associations with individual Scottish clans or families. Traditionally, tartans appeared only on woollen cloth but today you will find them on all manner of modern fabrics.

For this project, a bold, tartan pattern has been combined with brightly stitched medallions. A pincushion was chosen as the subject because it shows off both the technique and the fabric so well, and the finished article is more than a little useful to a cross stitcher!

Here, three pincushions have been produced using the same tartan design. Only two of them have been colour charted, however – the third is shown opposite in an alternative colourway. The two large pieces were worked on 11 hpi aida using different threads to highlight the effect that different colours can have on the same design. The small one was worked on 22 hpi aida, using the same chart, to illustrate how by changing the size of fabric you can alter the scale of a piece.

To use up oddments of aida, work a number of squares and sew them together in the same way as patchwork to make a cushion cover.

PLAYING CARD CUSHION

This project is an example of how, by borrowing designs and symbols from everyday objects, you can produce really eye-catching cross stitch results. The impact of this cushion stems primarily from the contrast provided by the alternating black and white backgrounds and the black and red of the symbols themselves.

Although plain blacks and whites have been used for the cushion, there is no reason why you should not achieve equally good results from a fabric with a small pattern, or even one with an interesting texture. To carry the playing card theme even further, when you come to make up the cushion try to find a fabric for the reverse that mimics the geometric patterns often found on the backs of real playing cards.

■ 046
■ 403

INSTRUCTIONS

The seam allowance throughout for this playing card cushion is about 1in (2 cm).

You will need six black squares and six white squares, each measuring about 4 x 4in (10 x 10cm). Using the waste canvas method (see pp. 8-17), work the hearts and diamonds in red on the black fabric, and the clubs and spades in black on the white fabric. You should end up with three of each symbol. Remove the waste canvas by damping it with a wet sponge and carefully pulling out the strands from behind your stitching with a pair of tweezers or your fingers.one at a time. Place a piece of thin cardboard with an 8 x 8in (20 x 20cm) hole over the square of fabric and, using pins, mark the outer edges (1). Pin and stitch together the 12 squares making up the border in the order indicated (2). Cut the centre piece square of fabric and then pin and tack it to your border. Stitch on the wrong side and then back the cross stitching with a suitable fabric to make it up into a cushion cover (see pp. 8-17).

MATERIALS

Fabric: 20in (50cm) white plainweave; 20in (50cm) black plainweave; 40in (1m) contrasting colour for the centre and back

Needle

Thread: Stranded cotton – 2 skeins of each colour. Use 2 strands for the cross stitch

1

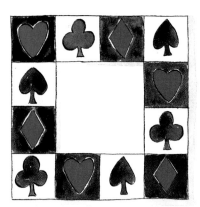

2

001
211
244
300
324
848

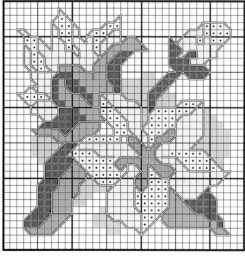

MATERIALS

Fabric (campanula): 6 x 6in
(15.2 x 15.2cm)
28 hpi evenweave

Fabric (domed): 6 x 6in (15.2 x
15.2cm) 18 hpi aida

Needle

Thread: Stranded cotton – 1
skein of each colour. Use 2
strands for the cross stitch and
1 strand for the back stitch
(campanula only)

INSTRUCTIONS

Number of stitches
(campanula): 32 x 30.
Finished design size: 2¼ x 2⅛in
(5.7 x 5.4cm) on 28 hpi
evenweave.
Number of stitches (domed):
48 x 48.
Finished design size: 2⅝ x 2⅝in
(6.6 x 6.6cm) on 18 hpi white
aida.
Prepare your fabric (see pp. 8-17),
find the centre of your fabric and
start stitching from the centre of
the design.

PAPERWEIGHTS

The thick glass of a paperweight has an unpredictable effect on objects viewed through it, especially the domed types that produce a distorted image of anything placed beneath.

The paperweights used in this project are available in kit form (*see p. 17*), and the two pieces of cross stitch illustrated were made specifically to fit them. The bases of both types are removable, allowing you to slip your stitching into place.

For the domed paperweight a classic style seemed appropriate, and the small – almost floral – effect of the stitching looks very fetching when the design is enhanced by the reflections within the glass. The flower design, taken from a 17th-century botanical study, seemed right for the square version. Like a crystal flower press, the glass keeps your stitching fresh forever.

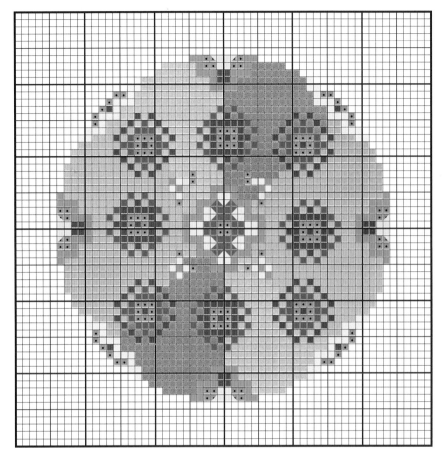

25		229	
112		235	
132		291	
160		316	
206		328	

143
146
149
246
303
305
9046
Gold
Silver

MATERIALS

Fabric: 9 x 11in (23 x 28cm)
14 hpi aida, white

Backing felt

Needle

Thread: Stranded cotton – 2
skeins each of the red and
green; 1 skein of each of the
other colours. Use 2 strands
for the cross stitch

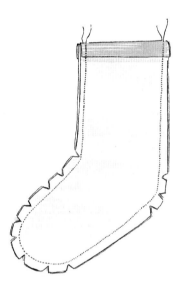

INSTRUCTIONS

Number of stitches: 97 x 71.
Finished design size: 7 x 5in
(17.8 x 12.7cm) on 14 hpi aida.
Prepare your fabric (*see pp. 8-17*),
find the centre of fabric and stitch
from centre of the design.

Place the stitched piece face
down on top of backing felt,
allowing ½in (1.25cm) all around
Turn over, hem the top and stitch
the piece to the felt, allowing 1
square outside the worked area.
Trim the seam and cut around the
curved areas as shown. Turn the
piece the right way around and
press. Stitch a piece of ribbon to
make a loop and, if desired, trim
the stocking with braid.

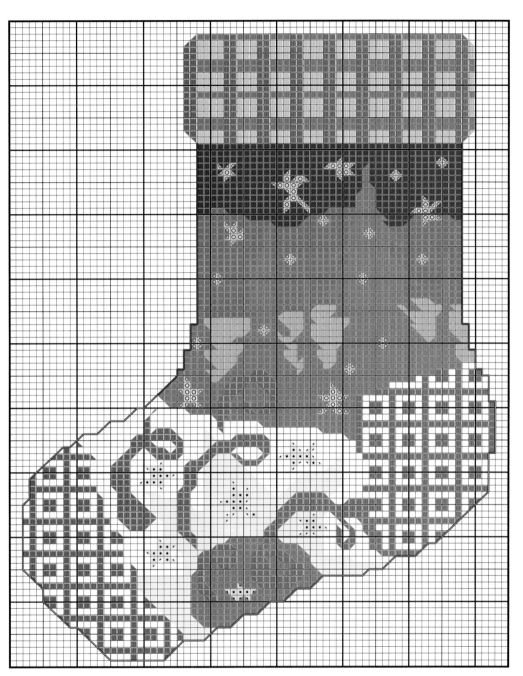

INTERMEDIATE LEVEL

CHRISTMAS STOCKING

The silver and gold threads of this
Christmas stocking keep the stars
twinkling and, if that is not enough,
there is a rich variety of patterns, too.

Working on this cross stitch project
should be enough to get anyone in a
festive mood. With something to look
out for every step of the way, and plenty of variety in the design, this project
will keep you on your toes.

If you want to increase the finished
size of the stocking to cope with larger
presents, all you need to do is stitch on
11 hpi aida instead of the 14 hpi aida
used for the one illustrated.

TEA COSY

This simple and very effective tea cosy has been inspired by a traditional patchwork pattern known as "tumbling blocks". Just like cross stitch, patchwork goes back a long time, and you will find literally hundreds of traditional and contemporary designs to choose from if you are interested, and many of these have successfully crossed over into other craft forms. And because patchwork is made up of geometric shapes, it is relatively easy to adapt and chart to use it for as a cross stitch project.

The most striking thing about a well-executed tumbling blocks pattern is that, no matter which way up you look at it, it always has a pronounced three-dimensional quality. This is an important factor to consider when choosing colours for your cross stitch version. To make sure you maintain the geometric ambiguity, it is vital that you select threads by tone, not just by colour. That is to say, you should choose a dark colour, a light colour and medium colour. If they are pinks, blues, yellows, or a mixture of all three, is not so important. So if you have a good eye for threads, and you have a good selection from which to choose, you could easily work this project out of oddments.

Any repeat pattern would look good on this tea cosy. Look at traditional patchwork designs for inspiration, and then get to work on graph paper and design your own.

MATERIALS
Fabric: 20in (50cm) 11 hpi aida.
Suitable backing fabric
Wadding and lining
Bias binding 1in (2.5cm) wide
Needle
Thread: Stranded cotton – 4 skeins of each colour. Use 4 strands for the cross stitch

▨	214
▨	216
▨	218

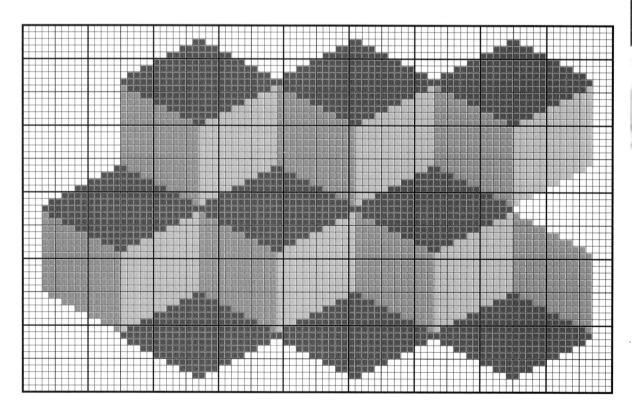

INSTRUCTIONS

Number of stitches: 144 x 112. Finished design size: 13 x 10in (33 x 25.4cm) on 11 hpi aida. Start by working the bottom dark line of diamonds 4cm from the bottom of the fabric. Level up the bottom edge by in-filling with the light and medium colours.

Work upward until you have finished the fifth line of dark diamonds. Using your stitching as a template, trace the curve for the corner and draw it on to the fabric, starting at the point of the end diamond. Turn the tracing over and draw on to the other side to mark the other corner. Continue the tumbling blocks pattern up to the edges you have marked, using quarter and three-quarter stitches (*see pp. 8-17 for details*) where necessary. Wash and dry the finished embroidery.

To make the tea cosy up, cut out the backing fabric and 2 pieces of wadding to the same size as the cross stitched piece. Tack the wadding to the wrong side of the worked piece and to the backing fabric. Place the worked piece on the backing piece, tack the right sides together and then stitch through all of the layers around the sides and top. Cut nicks in the curved seam, turn the piece the right side out and press.

Make up the lining in the same way, but without the wadding.

Place the lining inside the outer layers, turn under the edges and slip stitch them together. To finish it off, trim with bias binding around all the seams.

INTERMEDIATE LEVEL

OVEN GLOVE

An oven glove is used practically every day, and because it has to cope with hot pots and spilled foods it needs to be robustly made.

The pineapple was chosen as a motif for this glove because the coolness of the fruit seems a perfect foil for boiling pots and pans. Use this suggestion or select a motif of your own that fits in with your kitchen's decorative scheme. Whatever you choose, the waste canvas technique (*see pp. 8-17*) allows you to stitch on almost any fabric you like.

If you normally use a two-handed glove, then just make two gloves (one left handed and one right handed) and join them together with a length of the same fabric. If the glove ever gets beyond the easy-cleaning stage, carefully remove the material on the palm and sew on some new.

MATERIALS
Fabric: 9 x 14in
(22.9 x 35.6cm) calico,
plus waste canvas

Lining and wadding

Needle

Thread: Stranded cotton – 1
skein of each colour. Use 2
strands for the cross stitch and
1 strand for the back stitch

INSTRUCTIONS
Number of stitches: 63 x 40.
Finished design size: 5 x 3⅜in
(12.7 x 8.6cm) using 12 hpi
waste canvas.

Tack the waste canvas to the
calico, leaving plenty of room all
around for the stitching. Work the
design in the centre of the canvas
(see pp. 8-17 for using waste
canvas). When you have finished
the cross stitch, remove the waste
canvas. To make a mitten-shaped
template, draw around your hand
on a piece of paper and add 2in
(5cm) all around. Transfer this on
to a piece of cardboard and cut
out the shape.

Cut out the backing piece of
calico to the same size as the
worked piece. Also cut 2 pieces of
wadding. Place the worked piece
face down on the backing piece
and then place the 2 pieces of
wadding between them. Machine
stitch around the sides and top (1).

Cut nicks around the curved
areas and turn right side out. Cut
2 pieces of lining fabric and stitch
the right sides and top together.
Place the lining pieces (inside out)
inside the glove, turn edges in
around the wrist and stitch them
together. For a decorative finish,
hand stitch around the outside of
the glove (2).

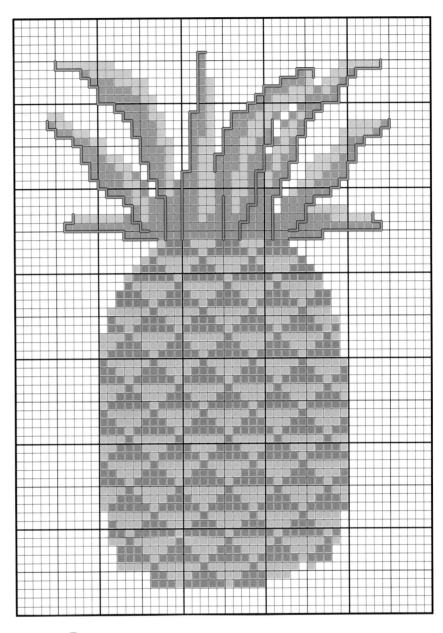

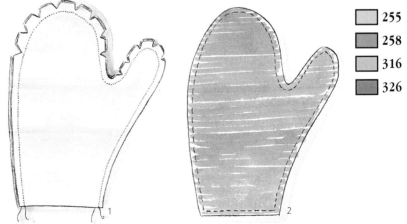

- 255
- 258
- 316
- 326

NAPKIN RINGS

In former times, napkin rings made of wood, bone or sometimes silver were commonly used. Sadly this habit has faded away, but with these cross stitched napkin rings you can revive the custom and present your napkins with a little of the style of yesteryear.

You can emblazon them with your initials or even invent your own family crest to use as a motif if you are feeling ambitious. For a simpler effect, just use consecutive numbers as in the examples here. If you have made the napkins from one the earlier projects (*see pp. 40-1*), you could always work the rings to co-ordinate with them.

Try taking the border style from one of the samplers earlier in the book or chose a tiny motif and repeat it all the way around the napkin rings. Alternatively, you can buy ready-made napkin rings from craft materials supply shops. These have a slot into which you can slip your stitched design.

MATERIALS

Fabric: 8 x 5in (20.3 x 12.7cm) 28 hpi evenweave

Cardboard

Needle

Thread: Stranded cotton – 1 skein each of each colour. Use 2 strands for the cross stitch and the back stitch

Sewing thread

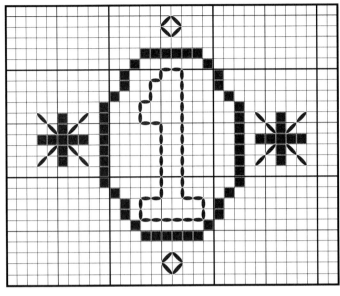

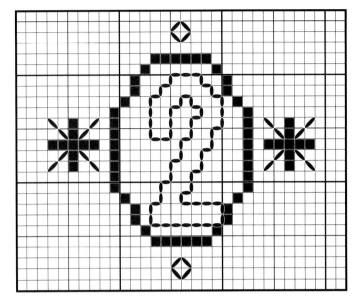

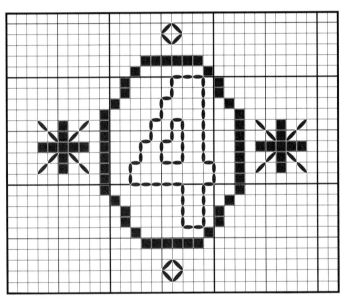

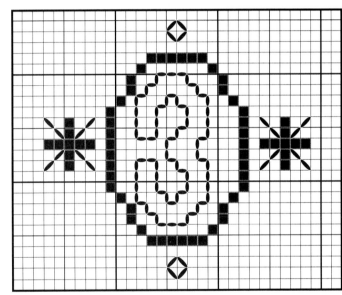

■ 403

INSTRUCTIONS

Number of stitches: 24 x 26.
Finished design size: 1¾ x 1⅞in
(4.5 x 4.8cm) on 28 hpi
evenweave.

Lay your stitched piece face down
and mark the centres – top and
bottom – with pins. Cut a piece of
thin cardboard – thin enough to
bend without creasing – to 2 x 6in
(5 x 15cm). Then use two strips of
double-sided tape to secure it
centrally over the design. Cut the
corners of the fabric as shown and
fold in to cover the card (1).

Sew the edges together along
their central seam, and fix more
double-sided tape as shown and
fold the ends inward over the tape
(2). If necessary, you can stitch
along the sides.

Now roll the card so that the
short ends meet and that your
design shows on the outside of
the napkin ring. Sew along the
edge where the ends meet using a
matching sewing thread (3) to
form the piece into a band.

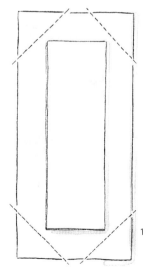

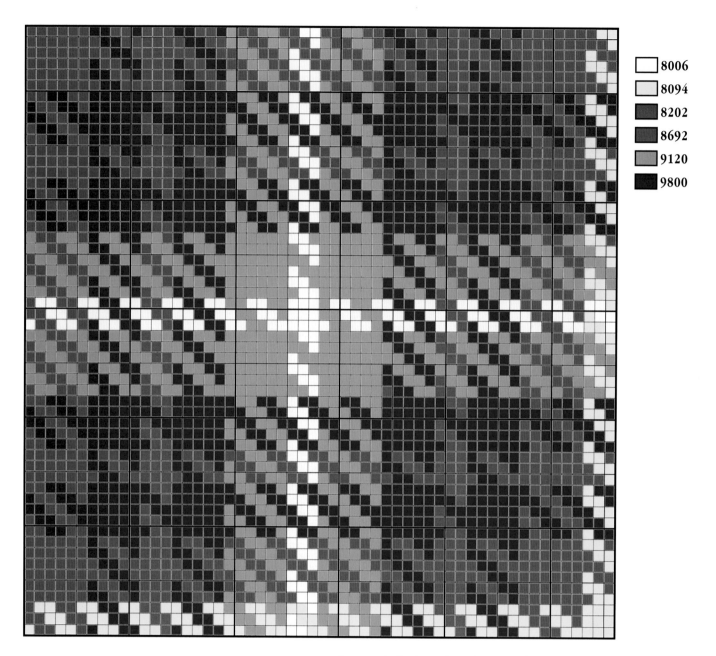

	8006
	8094
	8202
	8692
	9120
	9800

TARTAN CUSHION

Don't be fooled – this is not a piece of woven tartan. Because wool has been chosen for the thread, worked on 7 hpi canvas, this design produces a result that looks almost like real weaving – although, of course, this tartan has a very contemporary appearance.

Another factor that helps to give this tartan cushion design a decidedly non-traditional feel is the choice of colours. Following the lead set by the fashion industry, a range of extremely bright colours has been selected to give a modern interpretation of an age-old tartan design.

Although the design looks intricate, in reality it is not. Working from one corner outward, you will find that you can quite quickly finish this piece. If you like the effect it creates, and you still feel in the mood for more, you could repeat the process using 7 hpi canvas to create a set of matching cushions for a chair, sofa or bed.

MATERIALS

Fabric: 21 x 21in (53 x 53cm) 7 hpi canvas; backing material

Needle

Thread: Tapestry wool – 5 skeins of blue; 3 skeins of each of the other colours

INSTRUCTIONS

Number of stitches: 125 x 125. Finished design size: 17¾ x 17¾in (45 x 45cm) on 7 hpi canvas. Prepare your fabric (see pp. 8-17). Start from one corner, 2in (5cm) in from the bottom and one side.

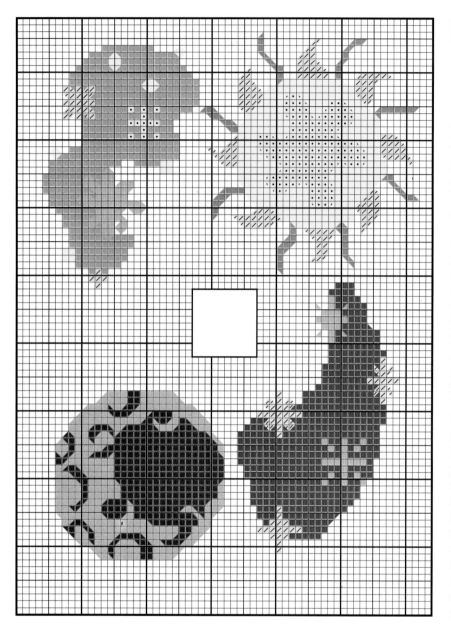

SUN AND MOON CLOCK

Next time you get the opportunity, take a close look at the dial of a grandfather clock. Often they have intricately engraved patterns or they may be hand painted with colourful scenes or motifs worked in enamels.

This project uses as its inspiration one such dial worked in cross stitch. As you can see from the photograph of the finished piece, this clock face features attractive sun and moon motifs, which are traditionally used symbols to illustrate the passing of day and night. But, although this project is intended to become a real working clock, it does not feature any numerals, so timekeeping will have to be approximate.

The working parts of the clock can be bought from craft materials supply shops (*see p. 17*), and they should also be able to supply a perspex cover to protect your work from dust and smoke. Alternatively, you can buy any similarly sized clock movement with a plain face and mount your work around its dial. If you want a more accurate timekeeper, take the appropriate numerals from one of the sets at the back of the book (*see pp. 104-5*) and experiment with graph paper until you have them positioned properly.

▨ 129	☐ 289	⦂ 300
■ 133	▨ 293	▨ 316
▨ 234	▨ 298	■ 400

INSTRUCTIONS

Number of stitches: 78 x 58.
Finished design size: 5⅝ x 3¼in (14.25 x 8.25cm) on 18 hpi aida.
Prepare your fabric (*see pp. 8-17*). Start by stitching the top left hand figure, leaving a generous amount of aida as a border. Place the other designs carefully, and when the stitched piece is finished, follow the instructions accompanying the clock for assembly.

MATERIALS

Fabric: 9 x 7in (22.8 x 17.8cm) 18 hpi cream aida

Needle

Thread: Stranded cotton – 1 skein of each colour. Use 2 threads for the cross stitch

INSTRUCTIONS

Number of stitches: 109 x 109.
Finished design size: 7¾ x 7¾in
(19.7 x 19.7cm) on 28 hpi
cream evenweave.
Prepare your fabric (see pp. 8-17)
and tack the outline of the tray on

to it. Stitch each motif starting
from the corner, making sure that
each one is carefully placed in the
corner of the tray area.

64

022
046
132
145
254
267
280
305
359
381
845
9575

FOUR SEASONS TRAY

This project turns tea time into a real occasion. For the flowers and leaves, the natural shades and earthy colours of nature have been taken as the inspiration, and the stitching is on a rich, creamy fabric. Evoking the feel of seasonal change, the foliage alters colour as it moves from corner to corner of the tray. The softness of this piece is achieved by working in 2 threads over 2 stitches of a delicate fabric.

When you have finished working the piece, there is no need to worry about spoiling all your hard work, since the completed stitching, which forms the base of the tray, is covered by thick glass to protect it against spills.

MATERIALS

Fabric: 13 x 13in (33 x 33cm) 28 hpi cream evenweave

Needle

Thread: Stranded cotton – 1 skein of each colour. Use 2 threads for the cross stitch and 1 strand for the back stitch

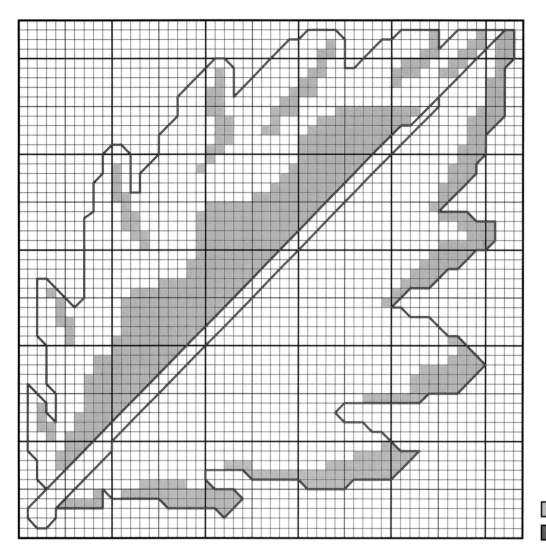

	266
	269

ADVANCED LEVEL

FOUR SEASONS TABLE LINEN

Leaves have long been among the favourite subjects of painters, illustrators, engravers and wood carvers. Whether it is just a single specimen or an intricate intertwining of leaves, there is something very pleasing in the shapes they form. Some, like the acanthus leaf, are used over and over again; others, such as mistletoe or maple leaves, evoke very specific responses in the viewer.

For this leaf-based cross stitch project, the delicate shapes have been worked on a set of fine table linen. The design is intended to compliment perfectly the four seasons tray that featured in the previous project (*see pp. 64-5*).

There are two elements to this set of table linen: a coaster measuring 5 x 5in (12.7 x 12.7cm) or 6 x 6in (15.2 x 15.2cm), with a central leaf design; and a 12 x 9in (30.5 x 22.8cm) place mat, which has the leaf design stitched at one corner.

By using the waste canvas method (*see pp. 8-17*) you could carry this decorative theme through to your other linen, such as the tablecloth, for a fully co-ordinated look.

MATERIALS

Fabric (coaster): 6 x 6in
(15.2 x 15.2cm) 32 hpi linen

Fabric (place mat): 9 x 12in
(22.8 x 30.5cm) 32 hpi linen

Needle

Thread: Stranded cotton – 2
skeins of each colour. Use 2
strands for the cross stitch and
1 strand for the back stitch

INSTRUCTIONS

Number of stitches (coaster):
52 x 52.
Finished design size: 3¼ x
3¼in (8.25 x 8.25cm) on 32
hpi linen.
Number of stitches (place
mat): 52 x 52.
Finished design size: 3¼ x
3¼in (8.25 x 8.25cm) on 32
hpi linen

For the coaster, work the leaves on the fabric, leaving at least a 2in (5cm) gap between each. Cut them out and hem.

For the place mat, cut the linen into rectangles large enough to accommodate a dinner plate and cutlery, allowing an extra 2in (5cm) all around for the hem. Hem each place mat. Cross stitch a leaf motif on each mat, positioning each one carefully in a corner. To make the mats more robust and hardwearing, turn the edges under and hem.

Alternatively, you can fray the edges by removing ½in (1.25cm) of fabric all the way around. If so, you will have to sew a line of back stitches right around the edge of the work to prevent any further fraying of the fabric.

MATERIALS

Fabric per panel: 20 x 21in
(50.8 x 53.3cm) 7 hpi rug
canvas, plus lining fabric

Fabric (cushion):
12 x 12in (30.5 x 30.5cm)

Needle

Thread: Tapestry wool – for
each panel, 4 skeins of dark
gray and 4 of light gray;
1 skein of each of the
other colours.

INSTRUCTIONS

Number of stitches per panel:
96 x 102.
Finished design size per panel:
13¾ x 14½in (35 x 36.8cm)
on 7 hpi rug canvas.
Border : 20 stitches deep.
Number of stitches (cushion):
70 x 70.
Finished design size:
10 x 10in (25.4 x 25.4cm)
on 7 hpi rug canvas.

ADVANCED LEVEL

ETHNIC RUG AND CUSHION

This design in warm colours against a
ground of cool grays was inspired by
the rugs and wall hangings often seen
in antique shops. While keeping the
character of the inspiration, the design
has been updated and would now hap-
pily fit in with a more modern decor.

In a world overflowing with mass-
produced objects, hand-made cross
stitched rugs have become highly
prized and appreciated, and now have
a correspondingly high price tag.

This project has been designed to
work either as a rug or as a cushion.
The rug is built up from four panels,
and one panel makes up into a complete cushion. For the cushion, the
design has been slightly adapted, with
the addition of a line between the
medallions. A border adds the finishing touch to the rug.

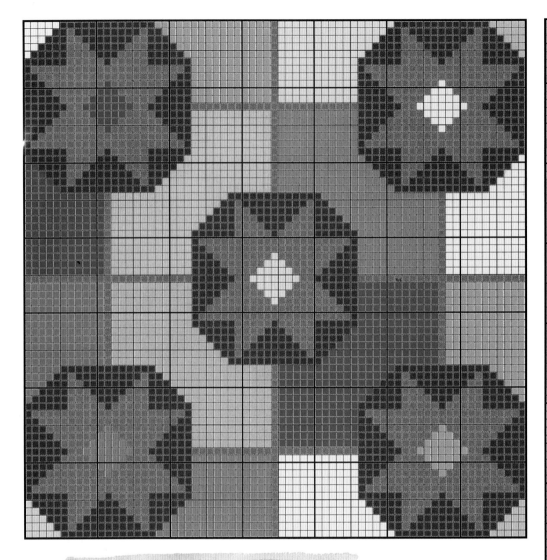

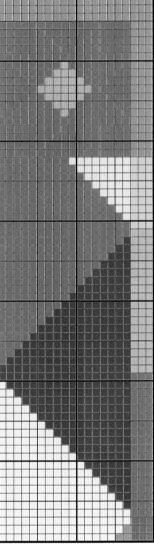

INSTRUCTIONS

Prepare your fabric (*see pp. 8-17*), find the centre of your fabric and start stitching from the centre of the design. Cross stitch does not generally distort canvas, so when your work is finished, all you will need to do is press the back of each panel with a damp cloth and leave to dry. If your stitching has distorted, tack the canvas firmly to a board, pulling it into shape as you go, press and allow to dry.

When you have finished the four, or six, panels, sew two of them by putting their right sides together and stitching with a matching wool from the back, using a running stitch. Fold back the excess canvas and press it flat. Begin working the border in one corner with the border star. Work from the chart to the sewn seam and then repeat from the other corner. Continue for the other panels and then sew all of them together on the back. Ensure all the excess canvas has been pressed flat with a damp cloth and iron, and then sew a lining on the reverse side of the fabric. When you have finished, the rug may need to be pressed on its right side and left flat to settle.

	8054		8242		8738		9402		9542		9796
	8100		8260		8786		9526		9792			

MATERIALS

Fabric: 12 x 8in (30.5 x 20.3cm)
22 hpi hardanger

Needle

Thread: Tapestry wool – 1
skein of each colour

ADVANCED LEVEL

MINIATURE RUG

There has been a great revival of interest in dolls houses and, particularly, in their furnishing and carpeting, making this a perfect project for a restorer.

Based on the previous ethnic rug project (*see pp. 68-71*), this miniature version successfully adapts the same charted design to a different scale, using rich, deep reds for the background checks and bright colours for the medallions. However, this is definitely an advanced project, and one suitable only for those with immense amounts of patience for the very detailed stitching called for.

INSTRUCTIONS

Number of stitches: 171 x 122.
Finished design size: 7¾ x 5½in
(19.7 x 14cm) on 22 hpi
hardanger.
Prepare your fabric (*see pp. 8-17*),
find the centre of your fabric and
start stitching from the centre of
the design.

Back stitch around the perimeter of the design first in order to give a firm edge to your work. Cut away the excess fabric, leaving just over 1in (3cm) at the sides and at least 1.5in (6cm) at each end. Turn in and hem the sides. Fringe the ends by removing the horizontal threads. Knot the fringing if desired, and then trim it to the length you want.

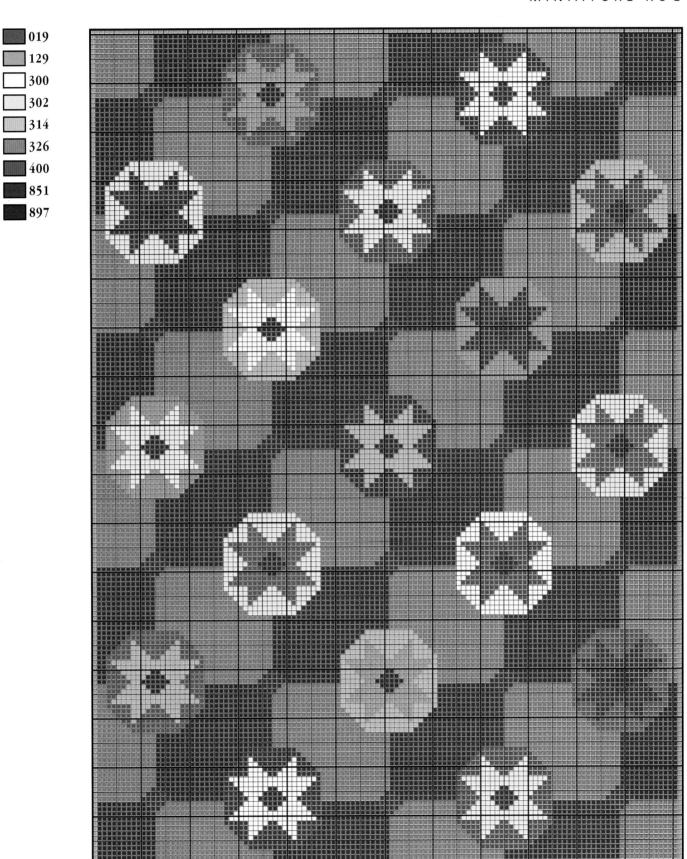

■	019
■	129
□	300
▢	302
▢	314
▢	326
■	400
■	851
■	897

PERSONAL ACCESSORIES

Ⓐ
- ■ 077
- ▨ 188
- □ 293
- ■ 1029

Ⓑ
- ▨ 038
- ▨ 261
- □ 868
- ■ 979

Ⓒ
- ▨ 038
- ▨ 261
- ■ 403
- □ 868
- ■ 979

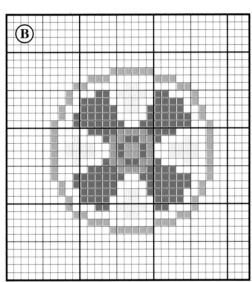

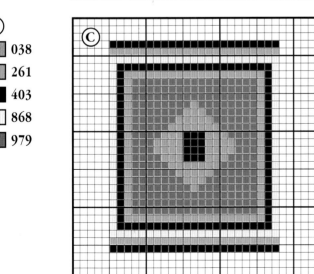

KEYRING FOBS

One of the unwritten laws is that keys always multiply. The ones on your keyring will simply carry on increasing in number until finally you need to split them up into different categories and bunches – house and car keys together, for example, and all those fiddly little keys that probably belonged to suitcases and briefcases you threw away years ago on another.

So as one bunch of keys becomes several, what do you do? You need more keyrings and that's where this project comes to the rescue. You could easily adapt almost any design from this book by experimenting with a higher count fabric to reduce the size of the motif, or just follow these charted patterns, which have been especially designed to fit into the type of standard-sized keyring holders commonly available from craft materials supply stores (see p. 17).

To find out how many stitches will fit into your keyring holder, lay the cardboard insert from the fob on the fabric, or some appropriately sized graph paper, draw around it and then count off the number of stitches.

INSTRUCTIONS

Parts of other designs in the book have been used for each keyring. They have had to be adapted slightly to fit the space – for example, the rectangular design from the border of numbers sampler had to be extended slightly. If you would rather make other choices, look through the different projects until something catches your eye, and then adapt it to fit the space you have available.

MATERIALS

Fabric: Fine aida, hardanger or evenweave – anything from 18 hpi

Needle

Thread: Oddments of stranded cotton or flower threads. Use 1 thread of stranded cotton for a delicate result

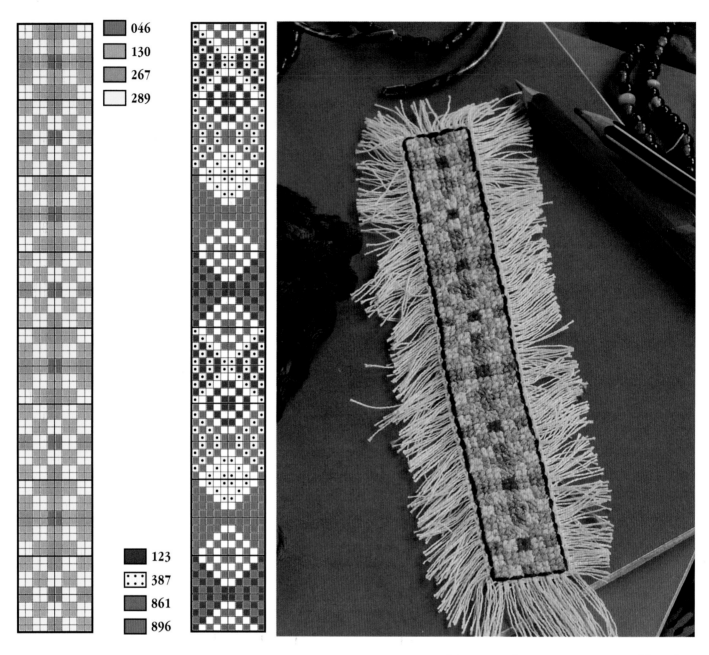

046
130
267
289

123
387
861
896

MATERIALS

Fabric (both wrist bands):
9 x 3in (22.9 x 7.6cm)
14 hpi aida

Ribbon or felt for backing

Needle

PVA glue

Thread: Stranded cotton or
flower threads – oddments
only required. Use 2 strands
for the cross stitch

EASY LEVEL

CHILD'S WRIST BANDS

Small pieces of cross stitch are ideal for using up oddments of material and threads. And the wrist bands you see here demonstrate that it is possible to achieve excellent results from cross stitch, even if you are a total novice.

To prove this, two nine year olds, who had never done any cross stitch before, were given graph paper and told to choose colours and design and stitch a pattern. Without any help, they came up with these two excellent pieces of work. Not only are their designs lively, showing good colour sense, they are also well stitched, have excellent tension and are even neat on the backs. If you have yet to try your hand at this absorbing craft, hopefully this project will inspire you to make a start.

INSTRUCTIONS

Number of stitches (both wrist bands): 80 x 10.

Finished design size: 5¾ x ¾in (14.6 x 1.9cm) on 14 hpi aida. To stitch the designs here, find the centre of your fabric and stitch from the centre of the chart.

To design your own, choose between four and six colours, decide on its dimensions, and mark the outline on graph paper. Back stitch around the finished piece to give a firm edge. Cut some ribbon or felt to fit and glue it to the back of the wrist band.

Choose stranded cotton in a colour that complements the design, and sew it through both ends (1). When you have enough, divide the strands into three groups and plait. Finish off with a knot and cut the strands to leave a tassel (2). Or, cut the aida ⅜in (1cm) from the edges, remove unworked threads on all sides to produce a fringe and fold the fringe back and glue it down. To hold the band on, sew on small poppers at the ends (3).

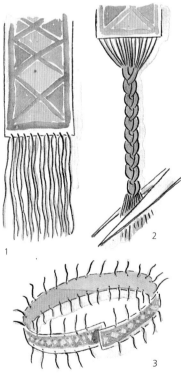

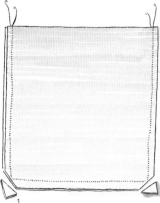

INSTRUCTIONS

Number of stitches: 68 x 75.
Finished design size: 11⅜ x 12½ in (29 x 31.7cm) 6 hpi binca. Prepare your fabric (*see pp. 8-17*), find the centre of your fabric and start stitching from the centre of the design.

Cut a backing piece the same size as the worked piece. Place it face to face and stitch around two sides and the bottom. Mitre the bottom corners (1), turn right side out and press. Cut 2 lining pieces 3mm smaller and stitch around three sides. Place the lining (inside out) inside the bag. Hand stitch the top of the outer bag to the lining bag through the slot in the wooden handle (2).

MATERIALS

Fabric: 15 x 8in (38 x 20.3cm) 6 hpi binca, plus lining and backing fabric

Needle

Thread: 2 skeins of 147, 265, 243, and 1 skein of each of the other colours. Use 6 strands for the cross stitch

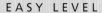

EASY LEVEL

CACTUS BAG

Cross stitch techniques have been used to bring out the chunkiness and spiky quality of the cactus motif used on this bag. The large stitches lend themselves to these characteristics of the plant, as well as making for a quick result.

All six strands of the thread were used so there is no dividing up to be done for this project. A piece like this is great for a child's first attempt at cross stitch and the subject matter is interesting, too. There is no need to use all four of the cactus motifs; if you want, you could simplify the design and decide to use just one of them.

If you decide to create a new species of cactus, stitch the pot first and keep a uniform thickness for the plant.

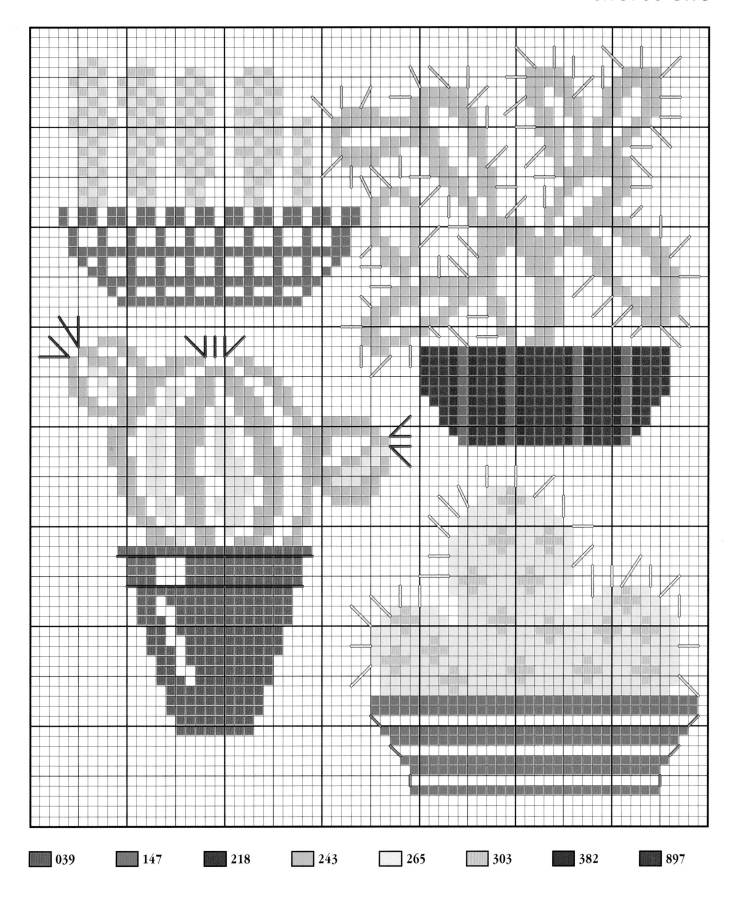

039	147	218	243	265	303	382	897

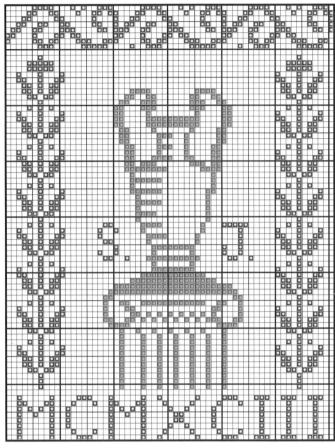

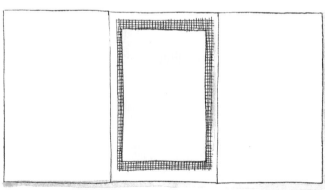

1

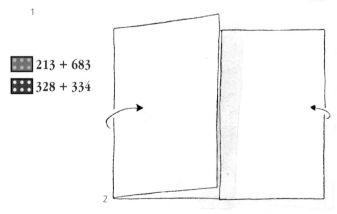

2

213 + 683
328 + 334

INSTRUCTIONS

Number of stitches (key pattern): 60 x 99.
Finished design size: 3 x 5½in (7.6 x 14cm) on 18 hpi aida.
Number of stitches (Roman numerals): 61 x 78.
Finished design size: 4⅜ x 5½in (11 x 14cm) 28 hpi evenweave. Prepare your fabric (*see pp. 8-17*), find the centre of your fabric and start stitching from the centre of the design.

Window mount cards for displaying your work can be bought from craft shops or you could always make your own.

With a shop-bought card, trim the fabric around your stitching to fit the aperture of the card allowing about ½in (1.5cm) all around. Attach the piece to the back of the frame using double-sided tape (1). Fold over the left-hand flap of the card and stick it to the back of the frame with double-sided tape, enclosing your piece of work (2).

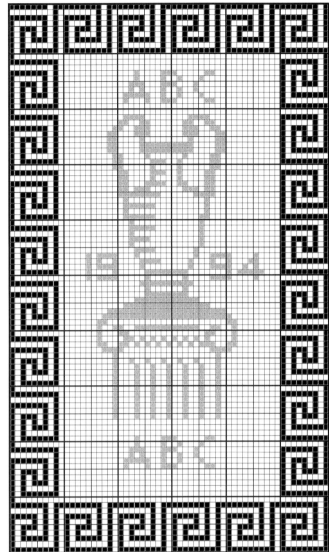

399

403

EASY LEVEL

BIRTHDAY CARDS

Many of the cross stitch projects in this book have been designed to make excellent gifts. With this same thought in mind, this project should give you some ideas for creating beautifully individual birthday cards, too. You can always choose a design to stitch that suits the particular interests of the recipient, or you can simply copy the ones illustrated here, which have a decidedly Mediterranean feel to them

and have been worked in a style not dissimilar to a traditional sampler.

There are two adaptations of the one design here. On one, a border of leaves includes the year in Roman numerals, which you will need to alter to suit the recipient. By combining traditional colours – two shades of green and two shades of a rust colour – the piece has taken on rather an antique look. On the other, which is worked in white, gray and black for a more modern feel, a Greek key pattern frames the design and it has space for a date and name.

If you like, swap the urn motif for a heart symbol and you will have an unusual St Valentine's Day card.

MATERIALS

Fabric (key pattern): 7 x 9in
(17.8 x 22.9cm) 18 hpi aida

Fabric (Roman numerals):
7½ x 9½in (19 x 24cm)
28 hpi evenweave

Double-sided tape

Needle

Thread: 1 skein of each colour.
Use 2 threads for the cross stitch

EASY LEVEL

BABY'S TOWEL

So that this book has something for everyone, here is a project for the smallest of tots, even if they are too young to stitch it themselves.

Bright colours and faces are guaranteed to attract the attention of babies and toddlers. These farmyard faces have been designed to be worked on to a child's towel for added fun at bath time. Many towels can be bought with aida panels already sewn in, ready for the cross stitcher, and this type has been used here to show off a range of motifs for youngsters.

For an older child, a flower motif might be more appropriate; and if you can find other items – such as baseball caps – which also incorporate panels of aida or linen, then you can try adapting any suitable design to suit the wearer. You don't have to worry about keeping the cross stitch out of the way of dirt and grime. Both the fabric and the threads suggested here are washable and colour-fast.

When you have worked on an aida panel set into a towel, it is sensible to sew a panel of matching aida on to the reverse in order to hide the back of your stitching.

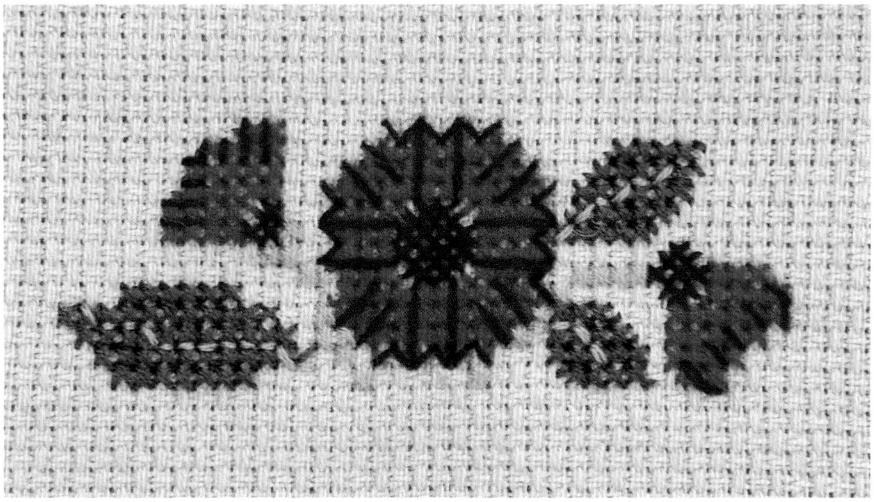

MATERIALS

Fabric: Towel with aida inset, plus matching aida back panel or other suitable fabric

Needle

Thread: Stranded cotton – 1 skein of each colour. Use 2 strands for the cross stitch and 1 for the back stitch

INSTRUCTIONS

Number of stitches: 113 x 23.
Finished design size: 8 x 1⅝in (20.3 x 4cm) on 14 hpi aida (inset in towel).
Find the centre of the aida strip and start stitching from the middle of the central motif. Carefully arrange the outside motifs in the space that is left, making sure that they are lined up accurately with the central design. You can cover the back of your work by stitching on a piece of aida, ribbon or other fabric cut to size.

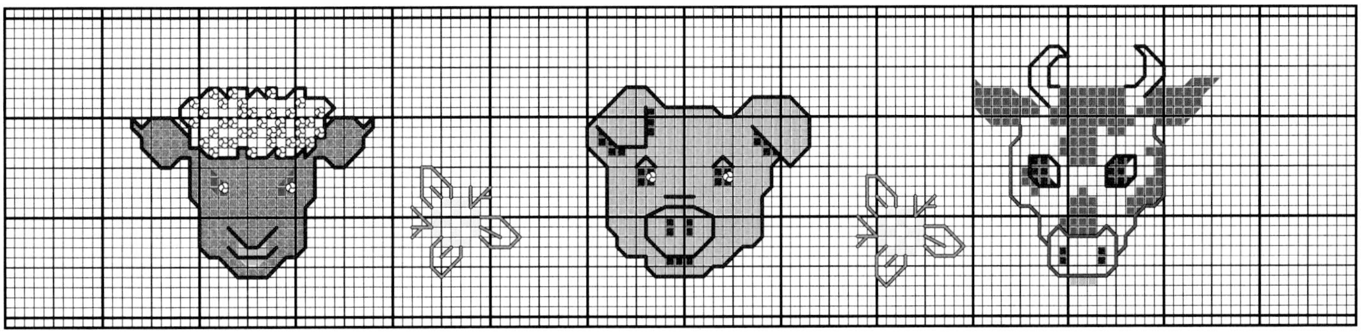

▒ **23** ▒ **258** □ **289** ▓ **370** ▒ **398** ■ **401** □ **926**

⁘ **712 Random French knots in one strand**

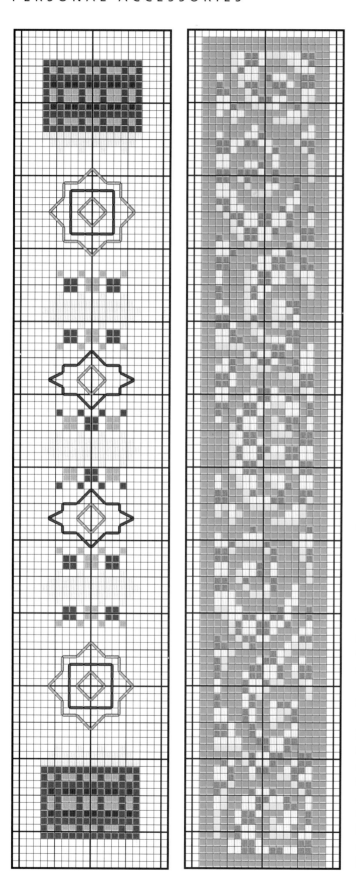

▨	926
▨	117
▨	046
▨	123
☐	885
▨	291
▨	895
▨	227

BOOKMARKS

These two bookmarks have been designed to give you a choice of patterns to suit your taste and also to give you some experience of stitching on a variety of fabrics. The livelier design has been worked on navy aida in red, white and blue, while the design on the canvas bookmark is reminiscent of the type of marbled endpapers found in some old books.

Due to their size, you could almost certainly use remnants and off-cuts of fabric for these bookmarks and, because the patterns are regular and repeating, it is an easy matter to extend them if you want. As projects they are not too ambitious for children to attempt and they would make easily posted gifts for friends far away.

INSTRUCTIONS

Number of stitches (aida):
14 x 115.
Finished design size: 1 x 8¼in
(2.5 x 21cm) on 14 hpi aida.
Number of stitches (canvas):
14 x 114.
Finished design size: 1⅜ x 11½
in (3.5 x 29.2cm) 10 hpi canvas.
Prepare your fabric (see pp. 8-17),
find the centre of your fabric and
start stitching from the centre of
the design. When this is finished,
cut off the excess fabric leaving
1in (2.5cm) on either side and 2in
(5cm) at either end.

Next, fold the aida bookmark in
half lengthways, with the wrong
side showing, and then stitch
along the length that has been
worked – but do not sew the extra
at the ends, since they will be
formed into a fringe. Turn the
bookmark inside out and then
carefully press it with an iron.
Remove the horizontal threads

past the stitching at the ends to
make a fringe.

For the canvas bookmark, mitre
the corners of the excess canvas,
taking care not to cut too closely
into the corners because of fraying. Fold over to the back and
then iron on the reverse side. Sew
the corners together. Next, sew on
fabric or ribbon backing. Finally,
over-sew the edges with 3 strands
of stranded cotton to strengthen
the bookmark.

MATERIALS

Fabric: 4 x 14in (10 x 35.5cm)
evenweave, navy aida, mono
canvas, plus ribbon or felt
for backing

Needle

Thread: Stranded cotton – 1
skein of each colour. Use 2
strands for the cross stitch and
1 strand for the back stitch
(aida bookmark only)

MATERIALS

Fabric: 1 sheet of 10 hpi
plastic canvas

Tapestry needle

Thread: Tapestry wool
or knitting wool – 1 skein of
each colour and 2 skeins
for background.

Press-and-touch fastener

INTERMEDIATE LEVEL

PENCIL CASE

This stylized leopard is perfect for the front of a pencil case. With some guidance, most children should have little problem working it through and putting it all together.

To give strength and rigidity to the pencil case, this project has been worked on plastic canvas. This material, in 10 hpi, is quick to work and has many advantages over fabric. One is that, because it is fairly rigid, it can be folded and will stay fixed in position. This allows you to form it into all manner of three-dimensional shapes – gift boxes, tissue boxes even jointed animals. As well, plastic canvas has the strength something like a pencil case needs if it is to hold up under the inevitable battering it will receive.

Once the leopard is done, work the other panels in different patterns using long stitches for speed. For a personal touch, incorporate the owner's name into one of the sides or into the back.

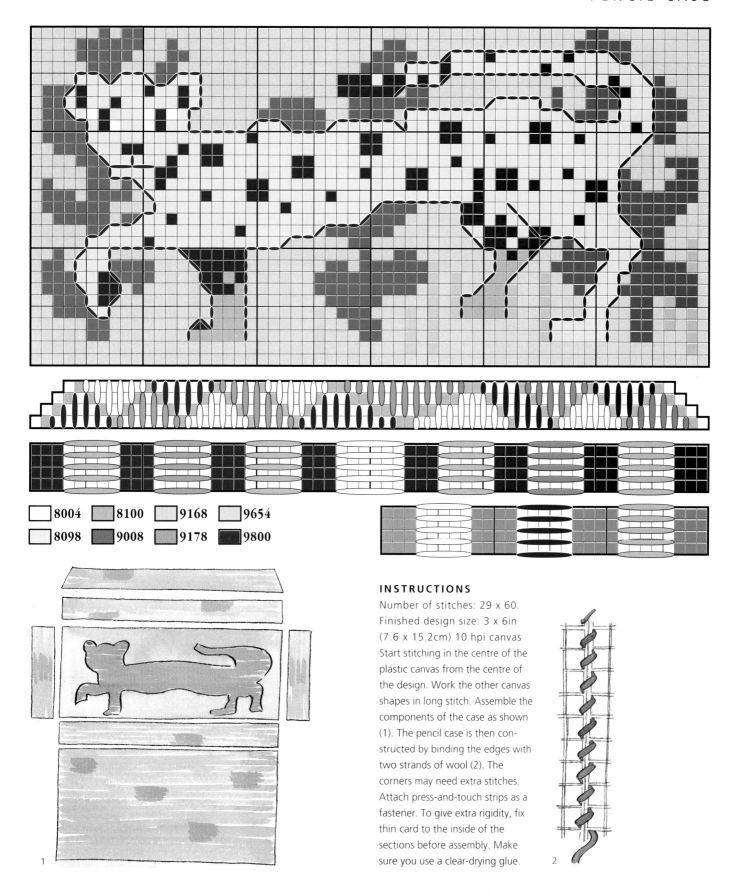

8004	8100	9168	9654
8098	9008	9178	9800

INSTRUCTIONS

Number of stitches: 29 x 60.
Finished design size: 3 x 6in
(7.6 x 15.2cm) 10 hpi canvas
Start stitching in the centre of the
plastic canvas from the centre of
the design. Work the other canvas
shapes in long stitch. Assemble the
components of the case as shown
(1). The pencil case is then con-
structed by binding the edges with
two strands of wool (2). The
corners may need extra stitches.
Attach press-and-touch strips as a
fastener. To give extra rigidity, fix
thin card to the inside of the
sections before assembly. Make
sure you use a clear-drying glue.

WEDDING AND BIRTH CARDS

The wedding card part of this project is designed to be worked in shades of pink and green and the birth card in pinks and yellows. To give the wedding card extra sparkle, stitched rings using metallic gold threads have been added. You can always add other details like names and dates in your own choice of lettering styles (*see pp. 104-5*).

To mount your finished work you can buy ready-made card mounts (*see pp. 82-3*)or, if you have stitched the design on a fine fabric you could cut your own mounts from thin card.

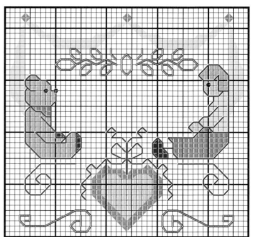

MATERIALS
Fabric:
7 x 7½in (17.8 x 19cm) 18 hpi aida
Needle
Thread: Stranded cotton – 1 skein of each colour. Use 1 strand for the cross stitch and 1 strand for the back stitch

INSTRUCTIONS

Number of stitches (both cards): 42 x 46.

Finished design size (both cards): 2⅜ x 2½in (6 x 6.4cm) on 18 hpi aida.

Prepare your fabric (*see pp. 8-17*), find the centre of your fabric and start stitching from the centre of the design. Add names, dates and so forth in the spaces. Work out any lettering and numbers on graph paper first and then work from the centre on the design (*to assemble the cards, see pp. 82-3*).

024
262
260
261
293
403
914
Gold
French
knot

MATERIALS

Fabric (each brooch):
3 x 3in (7.6 x 7.6cm)

Needle

Thread: Stranded cotton –1
skein of each. Use 2 strands
for the cross stitch and 1
strand for the back stitch

Needlework finisher

Safety pin or brooch pin

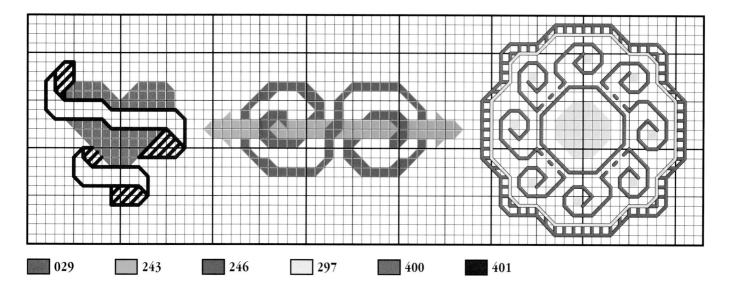

■ 029	■ 243	■ 246	■ 297	■ 400	■ 401

BROOCHES

These brooches make stylish personal accessories, and the designs have been devised to encourage those not too experienced at cross stitch to try their hand at something more advanced. You can either use the suggested fabric and thread colours to make up copies of the ones illustrated here, or create your own designs to use up any oddments of thread and fabric you may have.

The three designs here are a heart motif, a traditional Celtic knot in a verdigris effect and a wheel pattern. They are all intended to become brooches but you could just as easily turn them into hanging decorations, pendants or fridge magnet.

For a hardwearing finish, a special needlework finisher has been used to cover the actual stitching. This is a glue which, when dry, is completely transparent. It effectively seals the surface of the fabric and thread, keeping them free from fraying, and allowing you to wipe them clean if they should become dirty. Another advantage of using needlework finisher is that it will not dull the colours of your work.

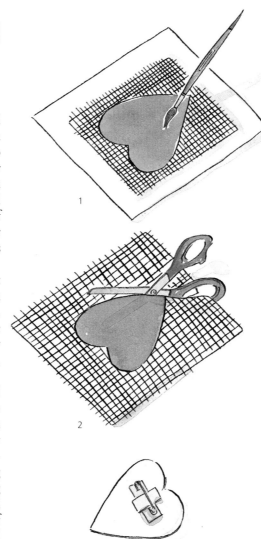

1

2

3

INSTRUCTIONS

Number of stitches (heart shape): 15 x 15.
Finished design size: 1 x 1in (2.5 x 2.5cm) on 28 hpi evenweave.
Number of stitches (Celtic knot): 10 x 28.
Finished design size: ¾ x 2in (2 x 5cm) on 14 hpi aida.
Number of stitches (wheel shape): 22 x 22.
Finished design size: 1⅝ x 1⅝ (4 x 4cm) on 14 hpi aida.
Work your design in the centre of your chosen fabric. Place your stitched piece face down on clean waste paper and apply an even coat of needlework finisher over and around the design (1). Follow the instructions accompanying this product. Next, lay the work face up on a piece of thin cardboard, smooth it over and leave it to dry. Brush some more finisher over the dried stitching and let that dry thoroughly, too.

Take a pair of sharp scissors and cut to within one square of the stitching, or cut the stitching into a simple shape (2). Fasten a brooch pin or safety pin on to the back with tape or glue (3).

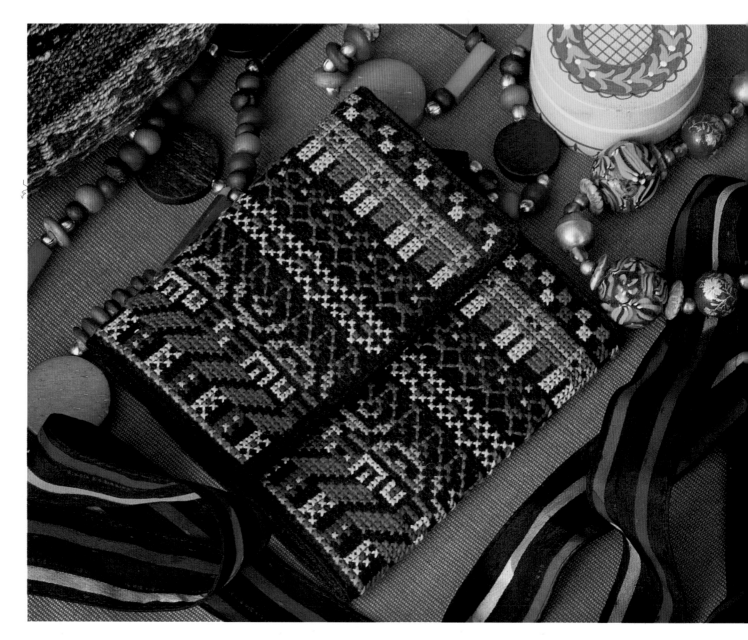

FAIR ISLE WALLET

This good-looking and practical wallet is a freestyle design loosely based on a Fair Isle pattern, but here it has been brought up to date by stitching on to a piece of black 14 hpi aida. The black fabric background gives this piece a solid look and lets the jewel-like colours really sing out. For all its good looks, this wallet is tough enough to stand up to normal wear and tear, and a press-and-touch fastener has been added. This is simple to sew on and fastens the wallet closed in an instant.

Although this design is intended to make up into a wallet, but you could easily alter its proportions and construction to make it into a glasses case or a cover for a personal organizer. If you place a circular or rectangular panel of different-coloured thread into the design, you could then add your initials or phone number.

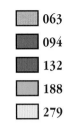

	063
	094
	132
	188
	279

MATERIALS

Fabric: 2 pieces 10½ x 5½in
(26.5 x 14cm) and 1 piece
10½ x 3½in (26.5 x 9cm)
14 hpi aida

Needle

Thread: Stranded cotton – 1
skein of each colour. Use 2
strands for the cross stitch and
2 strands for the back stitch

INSTRUCTIONS

Number of stitches: 56 x 130.
Finished design size: 4 x 9¼in
(10 x 23.5cm) on 14 hpi
black aida.
Following the charted design and,
leaving about a ½in (1.5cm)
border, cross stitch on one of the
larger pieces. When this is
complete, fold it over a hem all
around, leaving 2 squares of aida
as a border. Press it flat.

Fold over and press under a
hem on the second large piece of
aida, so that it matches the em-
broidered piece for size.

Fold over and stitch a hem on
one long side of the narrower
piece of aida, and then fold over
and press a hem on the other
three sides, matching the ends and
bottom to the larger pieces. With
hems facing each other, pin all the
pieces together and stab stitch
through the holes, 1 hole in from
the edge all around. Finally, stitch
press-and-touch fastening on the
ends as a fastener for the wallet.

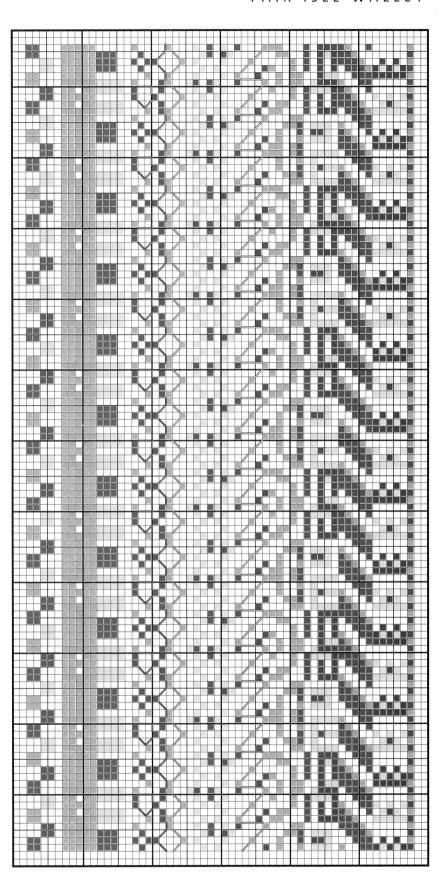

| | 001 | | 046 | | 169 | | 302 | | 303 | | 330 |

MATERIALS

Cotton sweater

Fabric: 8/9 hpi waste canvas

Interlining

Needle

Thread: Coton à broder – 2 skeins of each colour. Use 1 strand for the cross stitch

INSTRUCTIONS

Decide which motif you will stitch first. Cut a piece of interlining larger than the finished size of the design and pin it to the back of the knitting where you want the motif to be positioned. Pin a similarly sized piece of waste canvas on to the front of the sweater at the same point, and tack both it and the sweater together. Stitch the design through all three layers. Dampen and then remove the waste canvas, strand by strand. Trim the excess interlining from around the stitching at the back. Work the other motifs in a similar manner over the sweater.

With an evenly knitted sweater, however, you can simply work straight on to it. The stars and swirls have been placed in a random manner on the example illustrated here, but how you decide to position the motifs on yoursweater is a matter of personal preference. The same motifs would also look good worked in a smaller size on a shirt collar.

ADVANCED LEVEL

CELESTIAL SWEATER

The stars are always in fashion and cross stitched clothing is also very much in vogue at present – both on formal wear and for livening up casuals such as jeans and sweaters.

For the stars on this sweater, a galaxy of yellows, reds, blues and whites has been used and, mixed in with the stars, coloured swirls create the impression of solar systems far away.

Because the sweater used in this project did not have equal numbers of stitches and rows, the waste canvas method has been used (*see pp. 8-17*) to stitch on the motifs without distorting the shape of the garment.

MATERIALS

Fabric: Black velvet-style material
Needle
Thread: 1 reel Madeira Metallic Gold 33 No 12. Use 2 gold strands and 1 strand of 293 for the cross stitch
Gold cord
Gold beads

INSTRUCTIONS

Number of stitches: 63 x 63.
Finished design size: 6¼ x 6¼in (15.9 x 15.9cm).

Cut a circle of black fabric with a diameter of 17in (43cm). Turn in the edge and hem it. Using the waste canvas method (*see pp. 8-17*), stitch the design on to the centre of the fabric. When the canvas has been removed and the fabric is dry, divide the circumference of the circle into eight equidistant points and mark them with pins. From the 12 o'clock position, measure 1½in (4cm) down from the edge toward the centre and mark this position (point X). From here, measure 1in (2.5cm) to the left and the same distance to the right and mark these points (Y and Z). Repeat this from the 3, 6 and 9 o'clock positions on the circle's circumference.

Make a cord with some gold thread (here, 9 thicknesses of gold thread were plaited). Fold points Y and Z into the central X point and make a loop with the gold thread you have made. Use a pencil to get an even loop and repeat this process at the 3, 6 and 9 o'clock positions. Make loops without pleats at the other marked points on the circle's circumference. Sew gold beads with sewing thread around the hem at ⅜in (1cm) intervals and then thread the gold cord through the loops.

293 +
gold

ADVANCED LEVEL

EVENING BAG

Tudor ladies probably kept their per-fumed hankies in a drawstring bag rather like the one featured here. Before the introduction of the zip fastener, drawstring bags were used by all manner of people and for all sorts of purposes. Very large ones would have been used as suitcases, while smaller versions made ideal purses.

Today, this style of drawstring bag is more suitable as an accessory for evening wear. With this use in mind, the fabric suggested here is a black, velvety material, opulently decorated with gold beads and finished off with gold braid and metallic thread. The beadwork has been kept simple, but it would be easy to add or remove beads to suit. To make it a real dazzler, you could cover the bag with gold beads.

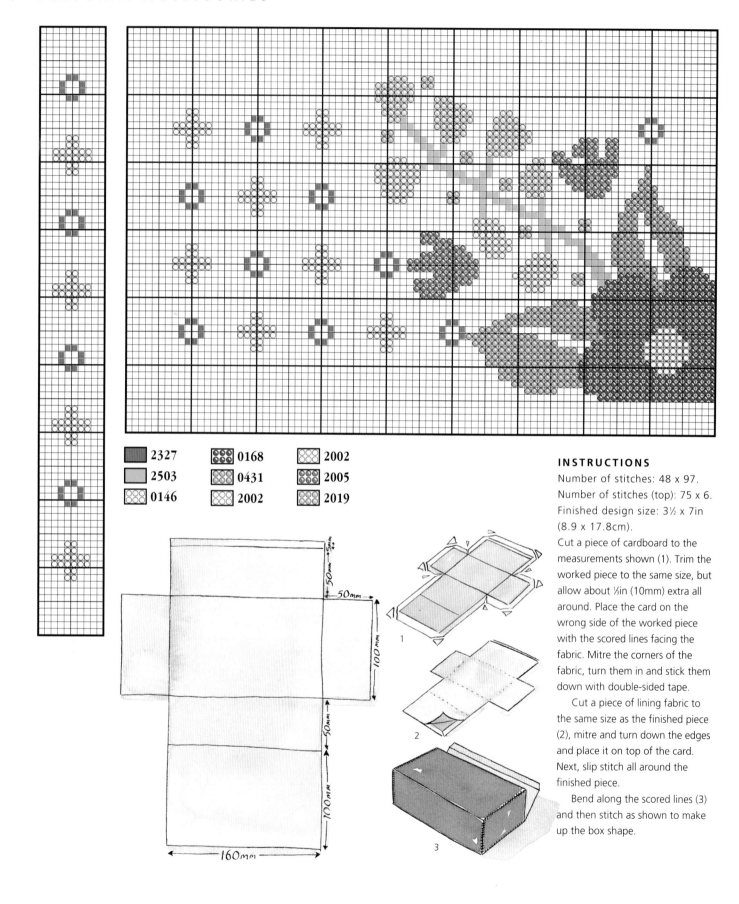

	2327		0168		2002
	2503		0431		2005
	0146		2002		2019

INSTRUCTIONS

Number of stitches: 48 x 97.
Number of stitches (top): 75 x 6.
Finished design size: 3½ x 7in
(8.9 x 17.8cm).

Cut a piece of cardboard to the
measurements shown (1). Trim the
worked piece to the same size, but
allow about ⅓in (10mm) extra all
around. Place the card on the
wrong side of the worked piece
with the scored lines facing the
fabric. Mitre the corners of the
fabric, turn them in and stick them
down with double-sided tape.

Cut a piece of lining fabric to
the same size as the finished piece
(2), mitre and turn down the edges
and place it on top of the card.
Next, slip stitch all around the
finished piece.

Bend along the scored lines (3)
and then stitch as shown to make
up the box shape.

100

BEADED CASE

In the years after the First World War, top hats and tails and long, slinky satin gowns were definitely "in" for evening wear, and this beaded case reflects the elegance of the twenties' style. Just big enough for a few pieces of choice jewellery, it is worked on a rich, creamy evenweave fabric for an understated, expensive feel. The pattern features a languid floral type of design, created by a mixture of beads for the flowers and flower threads for their stems.

The example illustrated here uses peach, oyster and other pastels, but you can buy beads in many different colours and lustres, pearls and translucents, depending on the effect you want to create. Victorian stitchers were also keen on mixing beads with their needlework, and this can produce excellent results with cross stitch.

When washing the finished stitching, take great care with the beaded areas. For a more subtle result, use threads instead of beads – try flower threads or metallic threads.

MATERIALS
Fabric: 17 x 12in (43 x 30.5cm) 28 count cream evenweave
Lining fabric
Needle
Beads: 1 x 500 count pack of each colour
Fasteners
Double-sided tape
Thread: Flower thread – 1 skein of each colour. Use 1 strand for the cross stitch

DINOSAUR T-SHIRT

Although dinosaurs have enjoyed an immense revival in popularity in recent years, they have long been a favourite with children. The dinosaur featuring on this T-shirt is pretty loosely based on a stegosaurus, which, with its row of spinal plates, would have been about the size of a two-storey house.

An advantage of cross stitching is that there is a wide range of good-quality, fashionable children's clothes to which you can add your own designs. Using the waste canvas technique (*see pp. 8-17*), this dinosaur has been stitched on to a cotton T-shirt, and when it becomes dirty you can throw it into the washing machine with all the other clothes.

If you like the result achieved here, why not work similar designs on to other articles of clothing as well?

INSTRUCTIONS

Number of stitches: 32 x 55.
Finished design size: 2¼ x 4in (5.7 x 10cm) on 11 hpi canvas.
Decide where you want to stitch the dinosaur design and tack on a piece of waste canvas in that position. Stitch the design and then remove the waste canvas.

MATERIALS

Fabric: T-shirt and 11 hpi waste canvas

Needle

Thread: Stranded cotton – 1 skein of each colour. Use 2 strands for the cross stitch and 1 strand for the back stitch

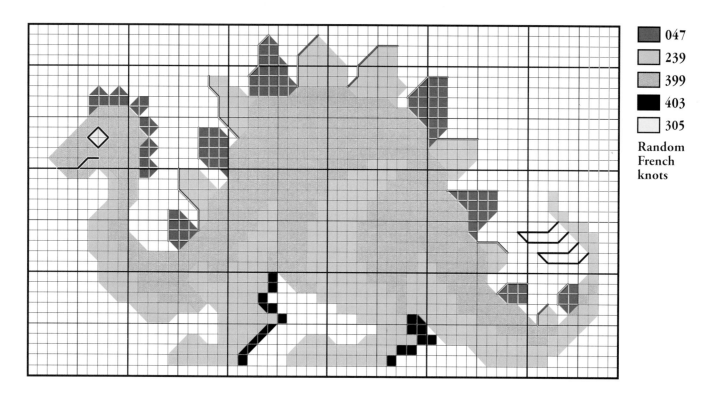

■	047
▨	239
▨	399
■	403
□	305

Random French knots

ALPHABETS

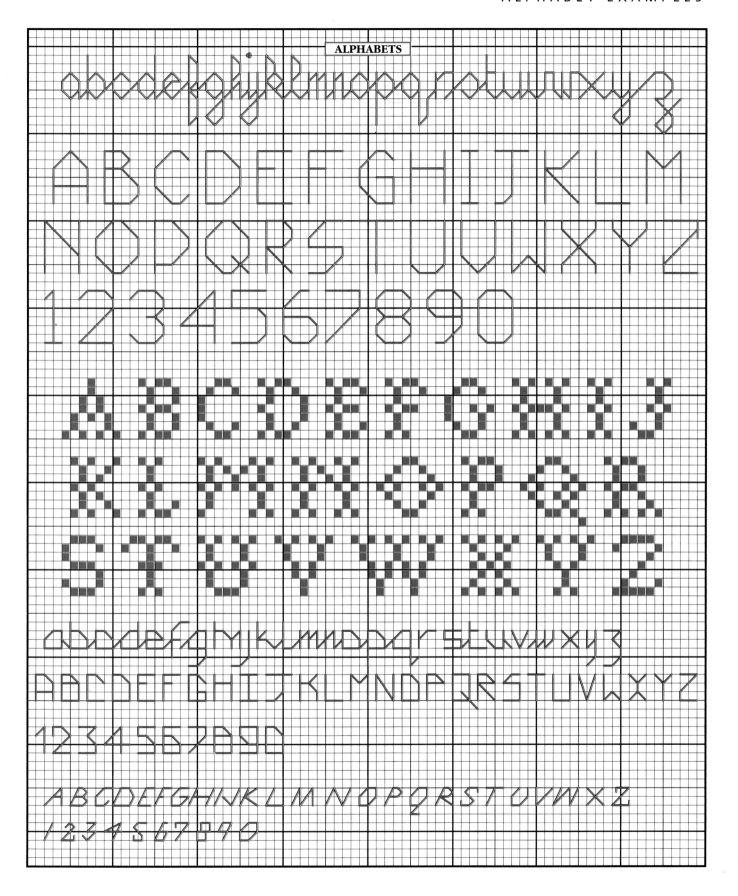

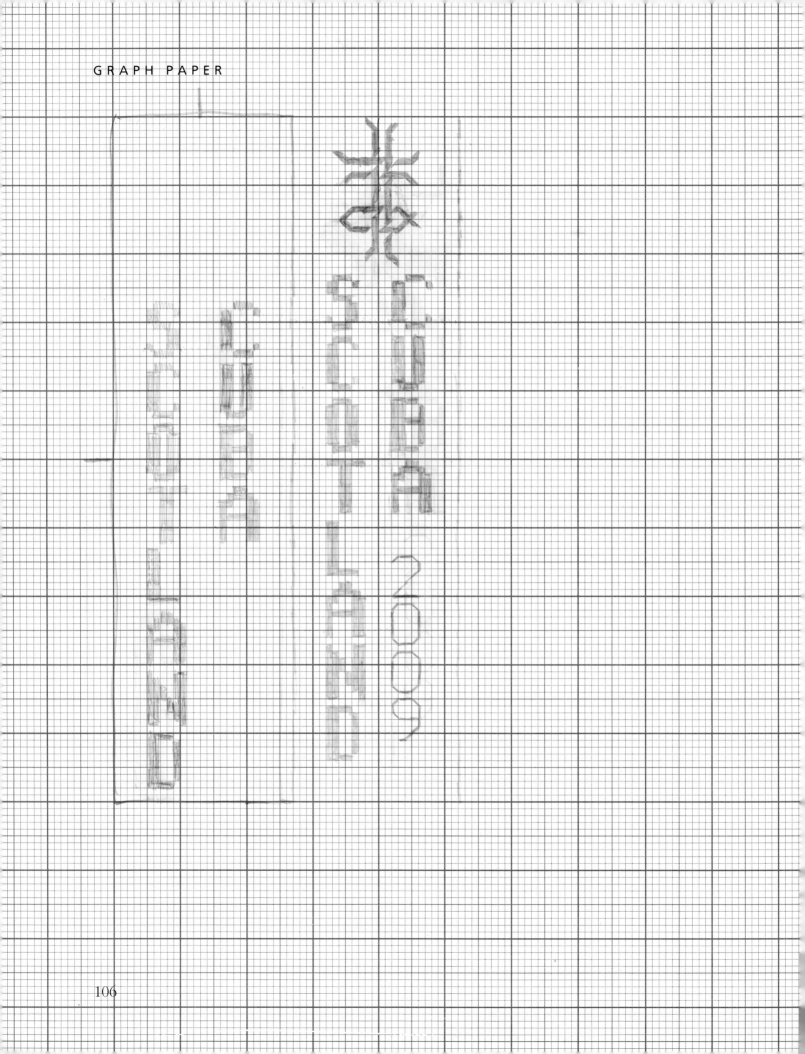

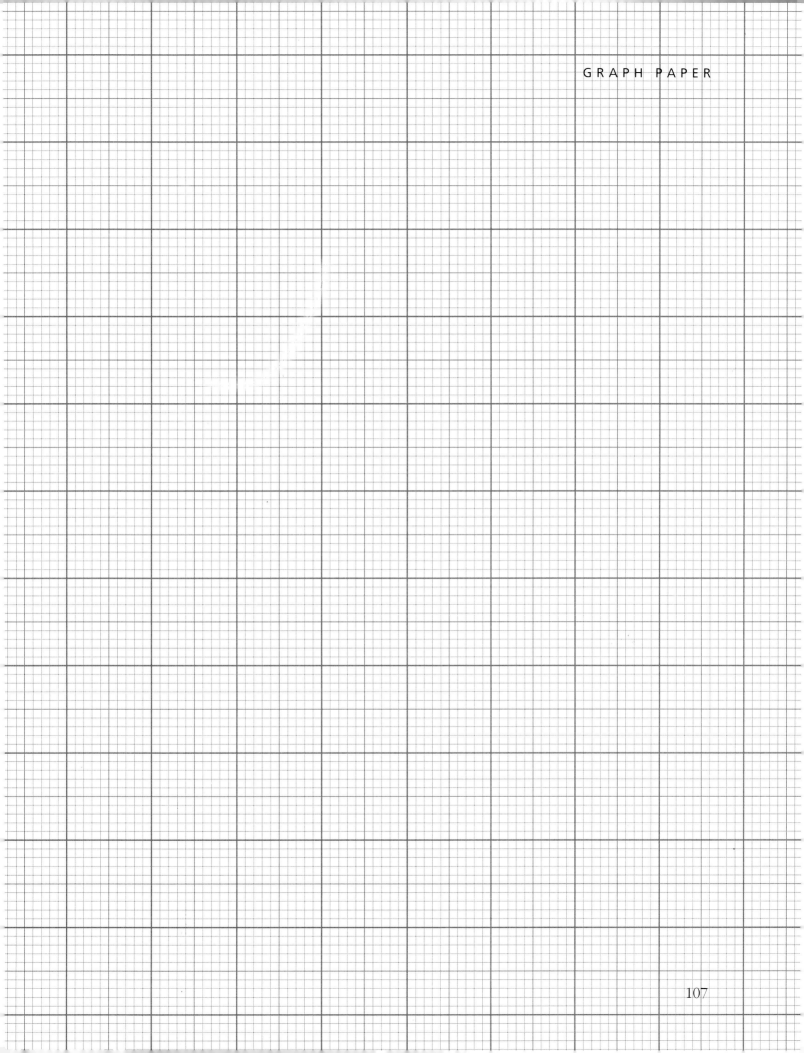

CONVERSION CHART

All of the threads referred to in the charts of this book are produced by Anchor. The other major thread producer is DMC. Use the following chart to buy DMC equivalents, but bear in mind that colour matches may only be approximate.

ANCHOR	DMC	ANCHOR	DMC	ANCHOR	DMC	ANCHOR	DMC
1	Blanc	75	3354	145	799	228	700
2	Neige	76	3731	146	798	229	700
6	754	77	3350	147	797	230	909
8	353	78	3350	148	311	238	703
9	352	85	3609	149	336	239	702
10	351	86	3608	150	823	240	955
11	350	87	3607	152	939	241	954
13	349	88	718	158	828	242	913
19	347	89	917	159	827	243	912
20	816	95	554	160	813	244	911
22	815	96	554	161	826	245	700
23	819	97	553	162	825	246	699
24	818	98	553	164	824	253	772
25	776	99	552	167	3766	254	907
26	894	100	552	168	807	255	907
27	893	101	550	169	806	256	906
28	892	102	550	170	517	257	906
29	891	104	210	185	964	258	904
35	3705	105	209	186	959	259	772
40	893	107	552	187	958	260	3348
41	892	108	211	188	943	261	989
42	309	109	210	189	943	262	3363
43	816	110	209	203	954	263	3362
44	814	111	208	204	913	264	3348
46	666	112	208	205	912	265	989
47	304	117	794	206	564	266	3347
48	963	118	793	208	563	267	3346
49	3689	119	333	209	562	268	3345
50	605	120	794	210	562	269	895
52	957	121	793	211	561	278	472
54	956	123	791	212	561	279	472
59	326	127	939	213	504	280	581
65	600	128	800	214	368	281	580
66	3688	129	809	215	320	288	445
68	3687	130	799	216	367	289	307
69	3685	131	798	217	319	290	973
70	3685	132	797	218	890	291	444
72	902	133	796	225	954	292	3078
73	3689	134	820	226	702	293	727
74	605	144	3325	227	701	295	726

ANCHOR	DMC	ANCHOR	DMC	ANCHOR	DMC	ANCHOR	DMC
297	444	369	435	860	3363	930	825
298	972	370	434	861	3363	933	3774
300	3078	371	433	862	3362	936	632
301	745	372	738	868	3779	939	793
302	743	373	3045	869	3042	940	792
303	742	374	420	870	3042	941	791
304	741	375	420	871	3041	942	738
305	725	376	842	872	3041	943	436
306	783	378	841	873	327	944	869
307	783	379	840	874	834	945	3046
308	782	380	898	875	504	956	3047
309	781	381	938	876	503	968	224
310	780	382	3371	877	502	969	3727
311	676	386	746	878	501	970	315
313	742	387	Ecru	879	500	972	3687
314	741	388	3782	880	951	975	775
316	740	390	3033	881	945	976	3325
323	722	391	3782	882	3064	977	334
324	721	392	642	883	407	978	322
326	720	393	640	884	400	979	312
328	3341	397	762	885	3047	1201	48
329	947	398	415	886	3046	1202	106
330	947	399	318	887	422	1203	57
332	946	400	317	888	420	1204	107
333	608	401	413	890	729	1206	115
334	606	403	310	891	676	1207	116
335	606	410	995	892	225	1208	52
336	402	433	996	893	225	1210	113
337	922	778	951	894	224	1211	91
338	921	779	926	895	223	1213	125
339	920	830	3033	896	3721	1215	122
340	919	831	612	897	221	1216	94
341	918	832	3032	898	611	1217	104
347	402	842	3013	900	648	1218	105
349	301	843	3012	901	680	1220	51
351	400	844	3012	903	3032	4146	754
352	300	845	3011	905	3031	5968	355
355	975	846	936	906	869	5975	356
357	300	847	3072	907	832	8581	646
358	433	848	927	914	407	9575	758
359	801	849	927	920	932		
360	898	850	926	921	931		
361	738	851	924	922	930		
362	437	852	3047	923	699		
363	436	853	613	924	580		
365	435	854	3012	925	970		
366	739	856	3011	926	822		
367	739	858	524	928	747		
368	437	859	523	929	813		

INDEX

ACKNOWLEDGEMENTS

THE PUBLISHERS AND AUTHORS WOULD LIKE TO THANK THE
FOLLOWING INDIVIDUALS AND ORGANIZATIONS FOR THEIR HELP IN THE
PRODUCTION OF THIS BOOK:

STITCHERS

KATIE BARON	DAWN HILL	LOUISE NEWMAN
KATHERINE BROWN	DIANA JONES	DEBRA PAGE
GEORGINA BRYAN	SARAH JONES	SHANI PHETHEAN-HUBBLE
CORINNE DAVEY	LUCY MACLAREN	SHEILA WHEELER
MARION DAWSON	TRACY MEDWAY	JACKIE WILSON
AMELIA FRANKLIN	CAROL NEVILL	

SUPPLIERS OF MATERIALS, ACCESSORIES AND PROPS

ANCHOR (COATS PATONS CRAFTS)
MCMULLEN ROAD
DARLINGTON
COUNTY DURHAM DL1 1YQ

FRAMECRAFT MINIATURES LTD
372-376 SUMMER LANE
HOCKLEY
BIRMINGHAM B19 3QA

THE DINING ROOM SHOP
62-64 WHITE HART LANE
BARNES
LONDON SW13 OP2

SPECIAL THANKS TO

ETHAN DANIELSON FOR THE COMPUTER-GENERATED CHARTS

TED FRANKLIN FOR HIS HELP WITH THE WRITING

KATHIE GILL FOR THE INDEX

GARY HOPKINS, ELIZABETH AND CYRIL JENKINS
SANDRA AND PETER, NICK AND CAROLINE, AND JENNY AND STEWART
FOR THE USE OF THEIR HOMES FOR PHOTOGRAPHY